D1409797

Diving & Snorkeling

U.S. Virgin Islands

David Lauterborn

LONELY PLANET PUBLICATIONS
Melbourne • Oakland • London • Paris

Diving & Snorkeling U.S. Virgin Islands
- A Lonely Planet Pisces Book

3rd Edition – November 2002
2nd Edition – 1992 Gulf Publishing Company
1st Edition – 1984 PBC International, Inc.

Published by
Lonely Planet Publications
90 Maribyrnong St., Footscray, Victoria 3011, Australia

Other offices
150 Linden Street, Oakland, California 94607, USA
10a Spring Place, London NW5 3BH, UK
1 rue du Dahomey, 75011 Paris, France

Photographs
by Steve Simonsen (unless otherwise noted)

Front cover photograph
Diver and French angelfish, Cow & Calf, St. Thomas

Back cover photographs
Spinyhead blenny surveys the passing scene
Cruise ships docked in St. Thomas Harbor
Diver at Congo Cay, St. John

The images in this guide are available for licensing
    from Lonely Planet Images
www.lonelyplanetimages.com

ISBN 1 74059 324 3

text & maps © Lonely Planet 2002
photographs © photographers as indicated 2002
Witshoal II illustration © David Lauterborn 2002
dive site maps are Transverse Mercator projection

LONELY PLANET and the Lonely Planet logo are
trademarks of Lonely Planet Publications Pty Ltd.

Printed by H&Y Printing Ltd., Hong Kong

Contents

Diving Health & Safety 31

Diving the U.S. Virgin Islands 34

St. Thomas & St. John Dive Sites 41

St. Thomas 42

Marine Life   109

Diving Conservation & Awareness   115

Listings   119

Index   125

Author

David Lauterborn

A Pisces Books editor, Dave joined Lonely Planet in 2000 after a decade in print journalism. He has since edited the Pisces diving guides to Fiji, the Red Sea, the Florida Keys, the Maldives, Honduras' Bay Islands, Belize, New Zealand and South Africa. Dave's first dive was off St. Thomas in 1981 as a wide-eyed 14-year-old, when he toured the newly sunk wreck of the *Cartanza Señora*. Seventeen years later he and wife Jill moved to St. Thomas, where they worked as both journalists and divemasters. They now live in Alameda, California, and are making plans to sail the world. Contact them at twoifbysea@hotmail.com.

From the Author

This book is a credit to Jill, who inspires me to new heights (depths?) with each passing year.

I'd like to thank my fellow divers in the VI for their generous contributions of knowledge and diving services. Thank you to the owners and dive crews at Anchor Dive Center; Aqua Action Dive Center; Barefoot Adventures; Blue Island Divers; Cane Bay Dive Shop; Chris Sawyer Diving Center; Coki Beach Dive Club; Cruz Bay Watersports; Dive Experience; Low Key Watersports; Scubawest; St. Croix Ultimate Bluewater Adventures; St. Thomas Diving Club; WaterWorld Outfitters; and White Dog Waters.

Special thanks to Pete and Laura Jackson, Bill Letts and Cristian Simescu. Thank you as well to Aitch Liddle and Sean Mckenna; Jim Oelsner; Billy Hurst; Joe Vogel and UDT Team 21; Coki; Lloyd's Shipping Registry; Tim Francis at the Naval Historical Center; Dave Burkhart; Mark Cullison; Zandy Hillis-Starr and Rafe Boulon of the National Park Service; Steve Prosterman; André Webber and Pam Balash; Michelle Pugh; Laurie Dunton; David Moir; and Dr. David Boaz.

My deepest gratitude to Roslyn, Deb, Sarah and Wendy, Emily and Gerilyn, Alex, Sara, Rachel, Brad and Justin—the swiftest fish in the tank. And thank you to Steve for his beautiful photos.

Most of all, Jill and I would like to thank our families for their love, support and continued patience with our far-flung adventures.

Photographer: Steve Simonsen

Steve Simonsen took most of the photographs in this book. Steve, with his divemaster wife Janet and their son, Jesse, has made the U.S. Virgin Islands his home since 1987. He runs Marine Scenes, a stock photo agency based year-round on St. John. His colorful Caribbean images have appeared in numerous books, magazines, newspapers and exhibits. Steve can be reached at www.stevesimonsen.vi.

Steve uses two types of underwater cameras: Nikon 8008s in an Aquatica A80 housing and Nikonos V. The cameras are loaded with Fujichrome Provia 100 and Velvia 50 films. For lighting with either system, he uses dual Ikelite 300 strobes or dual Nikon SB105s. For lenses, Nikkor 16mm, fisheye 15mm, Rectilinear 20mm, 24mm, 35mm, 55mm Micro and 105mm Micro do the trick. On land, Steve uses a Nikon F100 and an SB26 speedlight. Favorite topside lenses include 300mm f2.8, 80-200mm f2.8, 20mm, 24mm and 55mm.

From the Publisher

This second edition was published in Lonely Planet's U.S. office under the guidance of Roslyn Bullas, the "Divemaster" of Pisces Books. Roslyn edited the text and photos with buddy checks from David Lauterborn. Emily Douglas designed the cover and book. Navigating the nautical charts was cartographer Brad Lodge, who created the maps, with assistance from Graham Neale and Justin Colgan. U.S. cartography manager Alex Guilbert supervised map production. Lindsay Brown reviewed the Marine Life section for scientific accuracy.

Pisces Pre-Dive Safety Guidelines

Before embarking on a scuba diving, skin diving or snorkeling trip, carefully consider the following to help ensure a safe and enjoyable experience:

- Possess a current diving certification card from a recognized scuba diving instructional agency (if scuba diving)
- Be sure you are healthy and feel comfortable diving
- Obtain reliable information about physical and environmental conditions at the dive site (e.g., from a reputable local dive operation)
- Be aware of local laws, regulations and etiquette about marine life and environment
- Dive at sites within your experience level; if possible, engage the services of a competent, professionally trained dive instructor or divemaster

Underwater conditions vary significantly from one region, or even site, to another. Seasonal changes can significantly alter site and dive conditions. These differences influence the way divers dress for a dive and what diving techniques they use.

There are special requirements for diving in any area, regardless of location. Before your dive, ask about environmental characteristics that can affect your diving and how trained local divers deal with these considerations.

Introduction

Cloud-capped green mountains tumble down to white-sand beaches that kiss sapphire seas. Settle into a hammock and you could be anywhere in the tropics. But there's a buzz here absent from other Caribbean destinations, and amid the bright red royal poinciana blooms and matching roofs are slick reminders of the territory's U.S. mainland ties—from shiny SUVs to McDonald's golden arches. At the same time, the islands retain a ramshackle charm and West Indian languor.

More than 2 million tourists a year visit the U.S. Virgin Islands, many of them divers. Most arrive in St. Thomas, the cosmopolitan center of the group. It offers upscale resorts, duty-free shopping and the territory's best restaurants. The bustling capital, Charlotte Amalie, covers the slopes surrounding the Eastern Caribbean's busiest cruise ship port. In its harbor is the newest Virgin, Water Island (incorporated in 1996), whose handful of residents tootle back and forth in dinghies for their groceries and mail.

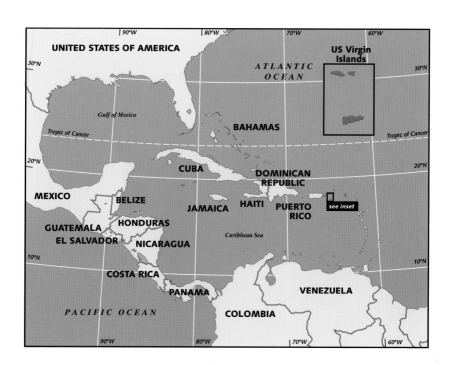

Two miles (3km) east of St. Thomas is the unspoiled jewel of the territory, St. John, three-fifths of which is protected national parkland. Regular ferries link its main harbor, Cruz Bay, with Red Hook, on St. Thomas' East End. The largest, most populous and remote island, St. Croix (pronounced croy), sits 40 miles (64km) south of St. Thomas. Its sleepy tourist infrastructure and rolling countryside speak to its detachment from the bustle to the north. Most of its accommodations, restaurants, attractions and diving are clustered around the two main towns, Christiansted to the north and Frederiksted to the west.

With bathwater-warm seas and visibility sometimes exceeding 100ft (30m), the Virgin Islands are perfect for student divers and novices. But there's something here for divers of all experience levels, including lush reefs, intact wrecks and abyssal walls. Sites off St. Thomas and St. John feature shallow fringing reefs and a host of interesting wrecks, while St. Croix boasts Buck Island Reef National Monument, Frederiksted's wrecks and one of the Caribbean's truly spectacular vertical walls, accessible from shore.

This guide covers 53 of the best sites the Virgins have to offer, including dives on **St. Thomas, St. John** and **St. Croix**. Site descriptions include depth range, topography and typical marine life. Following the descriptions is a photo gallery of common vertebrates and invertebrates to help you identify the marine life you'll find. To aid in your travel plans, there are tips on topside logistics and attractions, as well as comprehensive dive operator and cruise line listings.

Bambooshay (enjoy yourself)!

Charlotte Amalie overlooks St. Thomas Harbor, one of the Caribbean's busiest cruise ship ports.

Overview

About 120,000 people reside in the Territory of the U.S. Virgin Islands. Residents are U.S. citizens, who elect their own governor and legislature, but who cannot vote in presidential elections. Though the territorial flag bears the American bald eagle, the legend on license plates recently changed from "American Paradise" to "Our Islands, Our Home," perhaps best reflecting local pride and yearnings for a distinct identity.

Most Virgin Islanders are descended from Africans brought here centuries ago as slaves. Other ethnic groups include a growing Hispanic population, Caucasians from the mainland and "down islanders," who flock here from the Windward Islands in search of jobs. On St. Thomas' West End you'll likely encounter "Frenchies," an insular community of mostly fishermen and their families, descended from French Huguenots who arrived from St. Barts in the mid-19th century. Descendents of Danish plantation families still live on St. Croix.

Though the islands share one government, there are really two halves. St. Thomas and St. John share the northern half with the neighboring British Virgin Islands—a popular stretch of cruising waters among private sailboat owners as well as a favorite cruise ship destination. Well to the south, just visible on a clear day, St. Croix is removed from the other islands by not just geography, but economy and culture.

Water, Water Everywhere

The USVI comprises only 129 sq miles (334 sq km) of land. On such a small landmass, resources are finite. The islands average less than 50 inches (125cm) of rainfall per year, and frequent droughts make water conservation a very real concern. Two-thirds of the territory's freshwater supply comes from saltwater that has been desalinated—an expensive and environmentally unsound process. The rest comes from ground water supplies and rooftop cisterns. Visitors can help by taking brief showers and using operator-supplied rinse buckets instead of hoses to rinse dive gear. And remember the island adage, "In this land of sun and fun, we never flush for number one."

Geography

The USVI straddles latitude 18 some 1,100 miles (1,770km) southeast of Miami. The islands lie at the northwestern end of the Lesser Antilles, between Puerto Rico, about 40 miles (64km) west of St. Thomas, and the BVI immediately to the east. The waters of the Atlantic Ocean wash St. Thomas and St. John from the north, while the Caribbean Sea laps their southern shores and wreathes St. Croix.

About 60 islands and cays comprise the USVI, though only a handful of them are populated. St. Thomas, the territory's tourism hub, stretches 13 miles (21km) long and 3 miles (5km) wide. Two miles (3km) east across Pillsbury Sound is St. John, much of its 19 sq miles (49 sq km) protected within Virgin Islands National Park. A string of cays (pronounced keys) links the sister islands.

Forty miles (64km) to the south, St. Croix is the largest of the main islands, encompassing 80 sq miles (207 sq km). On the island's east tip is Point Udall, the easternmost point in the United States.

Geology

The Virgin Islands are perched along a seismically active rift between the Caribbean and North American tectonic plates. As the plates slid together over millions of years, the seafloor folded and buckled between them, forming deep trenches and steep walls. Though known for its hurricanes, the territory also regularly experiences moderate earthquakes.

The islands themselves are largely volcanic in origin. Seventy million years ago molten rock surged up through vents in the Earth's mantle, forming ridges that parallel the tectonic rift. These ridges are capped by steep mountains that rise abruptly more than 1,000ft (300m) above sea level. On St. Thomas and St. John the mountains drop to sandy shorelines, while St. Croix's highlands are limited to the northwest and east. The rest of the island comprises uplifted sedimentary rock, characterized by low-rolling grazing land.

Underwater, the topography bears dramatic witness to the geologic upheaval. St. Croix's north shore borders the abyssal Virgin Trough, which plunges several thousand feet within a mile of land. One-hundred miles (160km) north of the

Thatch Cay is one of a string of volcanically formed islands that link St. Thomas and St. John.

What Exactly Is a Coral Reef?

Animal, vegetable or mineral? Actually, a coral reef comprises all three. Corals themselves are animals, colonies of tiny polyps in protective cups of their own making. Each polyp has a stomach, a mouth and a circle of tentacles it stretches into the water to grab passing plankton. Connective tissues allow a polyp to share food with its neighbors, ensuring the colony's survival. Simply touching a coral can damage these fragile tissues and kill the colony.

Corals also harbor algae within their tissues. Like all photosynthetic plants, the algae harness the sun's rays to produce food, which they share with the polyps, receiving essential nutrients in return. A byproduct of this relationship is calcium carbonate, or limestone. The resulting limestone plates, mounds, pillars and spheres cap the reefs like icing on a cake, each new generation of coral growing atop the skeletal remains of its predecessors.

territory is the Puerto Rico Trench, which drops below 30,000ft (9,000m), the deepest point in the Atlantic.

History

Not much is known about the first people to visit these islands, a nomadic Amerindian tribe known as the Ciboney. They were followed by the peaceful Arawaks, who migrated up the Lesser Antilles from South America around 200 BC. Their culture flourished for more than 1,000 years, till the arrival of the cannibalistic Caribs (hence Caribbean), who ravaged the region in the mid-15th century. A subgroup of the Arawaks known as the Tainos survived in small settlements on St. John. They gave us such words as tobacco, hammock and cay.

In 1493, during his second voyage to the New World, Christopher Columbus sailed into these waters and named the land "Las Once Mil Virgenes" (The 11,000 Virgins) in honor of St. Ursula and her martyred virgins of legendary beauty. When his men went ashore at St. Croix's Salt River Bay in search of fresh water, the Caribs gave them a hostile reception. Subsequent warfare and disease decimated the Indians, and by the time Europeans began to settle the islands in the 17th century, few of them remained.

The busy waters and waning Spanish strength soon attracted pirates and privateers, who used the Virgin Islands both as a safe haven and as a base from which to raid gold-laden Spanish galleons sailing home from the Americas. Their mark lingers in such place names as Blackbeard's Castle on St. Thomas and Sir Francis Drake Channel east of St. John.

The British settled the islands east of St. John and still hold dominion there today. The Danes colonized St. Thomas and St. John, while St. Croix changed hands between the British, Dutch, Spanish and French. Plagued by wars, piracy and religious conflicts, France abandoned its claim on St. Croix, selling the island to the Danish West India & Guinea Co. in 1733. The Danish West Indies soon became a center of commerce, sugarcane farming and the burgeoning slave trade.

Denmark flirted with abolition during the first half of the 19th century, but it was a slave rebellion on St. Croix in 1848 that eventually forced the issue. The plantations were already in decline following soil exhaustion and a fall in sugar prices. The economic downturn accelerated in the wake of abolition, and the Danes were eager to find a buyer.

Realizing the islands' strategic importance as a shipping route to the Panama Canal, the U.S. bought them from Denmark on March 31, 1917, for $25 million in gold. The U.S. Navy administered the territory for the next 14 years. While the period brought material improvements, islanders themselves were largely ignored. They were finally granted U.S. citizenship in 1927, and the territory was turned over to civil rule in 1931. The Organic Act of 1936 extended voting rights to all English-speaking residents 21 and over.

By WWII development was in full swing. Military construction meant jobs to the islanders. It also fixed the territory in the minds of visiting American service-men, who would return after the war to vacation. In 1950 Gov. Morris de Castro kicked off an aggressive campaign to boost tourism, and when the U.S. banned American travel to Cuba in 1959, vacationers flocked to the USVI. Tax incentives drew Hess Oil and other manufacturing operations to the territory in the 1960s, further boosting the local economy.

Today the tourism industry employs the majority of the workforce and accounts for more than 70% of the gross domestic product. And there are recent signs of diversification into light industry, international business and financial services. But prosperity has brought with it growing pains, in the form of overcrowding, pollution, high crime rates and political corruption. While the per capita income is among the highest in the Caribbean, the government remains the single biggest employer. A series of devastating hurricanes since 1989 have only added to the territory's woes, leaving it with $1 billion in federal debt. Recovery efforts center on fiscal responsibility and education reform.

Sugar mill ruins dot St. Croix's rural landscape.

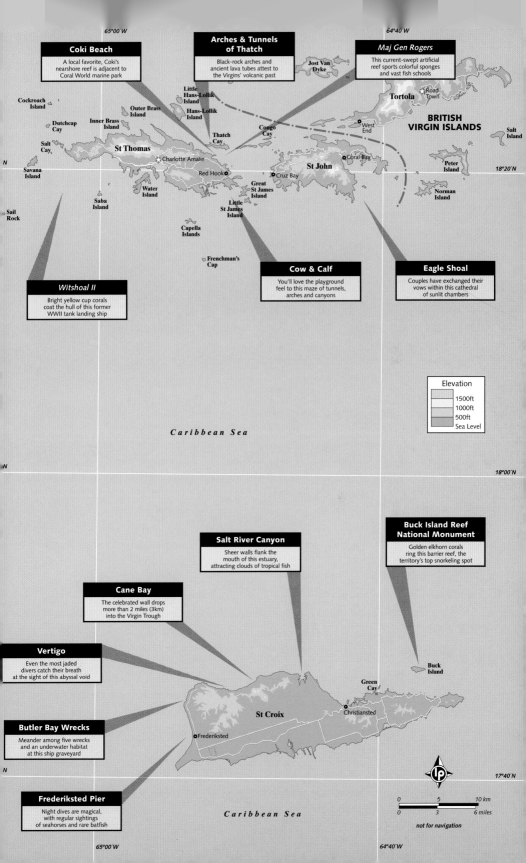

65°00'W

64°40'W

Coki Beach
A local favorite, Coki's nearshore reef is adjacent to Coral World marine park

Arches & Tunnels of Thatch
Black-rock arches and ancient lava tubes attest to the Virgins' volcanic past

Maj Gen Rogers
This current-swept artificial reef sports colorful sponges and vast fish schools

Jost Van Dyke

Tortola
Road Town

BRITISH VIRGIN ISLANDS

Cockroach Island

Outer Brass Island

Little Hans-Lollik Island

Salt Island

Dutchcap Cay

Inner Brass Island

Hans-Lollik Island

West End

Salt Cay

Thatch Cay

Congo Cay

N

St Thomas

Charlotte Amalie

Coral Bay

Peter Island

Savana Island

Red Hook

St John

18°20'N

Sail Rock

Saba Island

Water Island

Cruz Bay

Great St James Island

Norman Island

Little St James Island

Capella Islands

Frenchman's Cap

Witshoal II
Bright yellow cup corals coat the hull of this former WWII tank landing ship

Cow & Calf
You'll love the playground feel to this maze of tunnels, arches and canyons

Eagle Shoal
Couples have exchanged their vows within this cathedral of sunlit chambers

Elevation

1500ft
1000ft
500ft
Sea Level

Caribbean Sea

N
18°00'N

Buck Island Reef National Monument
Golden elkhorn corals ring this barrier reef, the territory's top snorkeling spot

Salt River Canyon
Sheer walls flank the mouth of this estuary, attracting clouds of tropical fish

Cane Bay
The celebrated wall drops more than 2 miles (3km) into the Virgin Trough

Vertigo
Even the most jaded divers catch their breath at the sight of this abyssal void

Green Cay

Buck Island

Christiansted

St Croix

Butler Bay Wrecks
Meander among five wrecks and an underwater habitat at this ship graveyard

Frederiksted

N
17°40'N

Frederiksted Pier
Night dives are magical, with regular sightings of seahorses and rare batfish

Caribbean Sea

0   5   10 km
0   3   6 miles

not for navigation

65°00'W
64°40'W

Practicalities

Climate

The climate in the Virgin Islands is consistently sunny and mild year-round, the only real change arriving with hurricane season (typically June through November). Average temperatures range from the mid-70s Fahrenheit (low-20s Celsius) in winter to the mid-80s Fahrenheit (mid-20s Celsius) in summer. Lows rarely dip below 65°F (18°C), while summer highs seldom break 90°F (32°C). Steady easterly trade winds temper humidity.

In the Path of Hurricanes

No doubt awed by the power of tropical storms, Taino Indians named the cyclones after their god of malevolence, Hurakán. The storms continue to play a major role in the history of these islands.

In September 1989 Hurricane Hugo caused widespread destruction on St. Croix, leaving much of its population homeless. In September 1995 hurricanes Luis and Marilyn struck St. Thomas, killing several people and causing billions of dollars in damage. The Federal Emergency Management Agency stepped in with temporary housing and several hundred million dollars in disaster relief loans. Years later, trademark blue FEMA tarps still cover some roofs, and the debt remains.

While more recent storms have been relative "salad shooters" in comparison, the territory braces for the worst every hurricane season, praying for mercy during the annual Hurricane Supplication Day in July and giving thanks for being spared (wholly or in part) on Hurricane Thanksgiving Day in October.

In 1989 Hurricane Hugo wreaked havoc on the territory.

High season, December to April, is typically dry and sunny, followed by a period of intense rainfall in late April and May. The wettest months are August through November, when the territory receives more than half its annual rainfall. Brief tropical showers are common year-round, though they pass quickly, leaving clear sunny skies. While hurricane season itself is largely unpredictable, there is a very good watch system in place, and warnings precede the storms by several days.

See Diving in the U.S. Virgin Islands (page 34) for information on diving conditions.

Language

English is the official language, though native West Indians also speak Creole, a folksy pidgin English mixed with phrases from several languages. There's a growing Spanish-speaking population, especially on St. Croix, and Danish is still used for place names and such common terms as street, or *gade* (pronounced gah-dah).

Local Word Dem

Following are some Creole expressions and usage you may hear:

OK	hello
gone I	goodbye
dem	more than one (e.g., "turtle dem")
duppy/jumbie	spirit or ghost
limin'	relaxing
mash up	car accident
pistarkle	a noisy free-for-all
galliwasp	lizardfish
katy	reef butterflyfish
old wife	queen triggerfish

Getting There

The majority of visitors to the territory arrive by cruise ship. Ships dock at the West Indian Co. dock and Crown Bay dock on St. Thomas and the Frederiksted Pier on St. Croix. On busy days ships are anchored off all three major islands. See Listings (pages 123-124) for cruise line contact information.

Two international airports serve the territory—Cyril E. King Airport on St. Thomas and Henry E. Rohlsen Airport on St. Croix. There is no airport on St. John. Airlines offering direct flights from the U.S. mainland include American, Delta, Continental, United and US Airways. Connecting flights are available from Canada, Europe, South America and the Far East. Several airlines offer commuter flights from Puerto Rico and other Caribbean destinations, including Air St. Thomas, Air Sunshine, American Eagle, Cape Air, LIAT and Seaborne Airlines. There are also regular daily flights between St. Thomas and St. Croix.

Visitors to St. John fly into St. Thomas, then hop a taxi to the Edward W. Blyden Marine Terminal on Waterfront in Charlotte Amalie. Scheduled ferries operate six times daily to Cruz Bay on St. John. Some resorts have their own boats and will arrange your transfer.

Gateway City – Charlotte Amalie

With a population approaching 15,000, Charlotte Amalie (uh-MALL-yuh) is the territory's capital and the Eastern Caribbean's busiest cruise ship port. Residents simply refer to it as "town." Its red-roofed buildings surround St. Thomas Harbor, ringed by steep mountains and dotted with sailboats and cruise ships. In the middle of the bay are two small islands, Water and Hassel.

Veterans Drive (known locally as Waterfront) skirts the bay. Anchoring the east end are the West Indian Co. cruise ship dock and adjacent Havensight Mall, home to the bulk of duty-free shops. Heading west toward town, you'll first reach the lime-green Legislature building and red stone walls of Fort Christian, a holdover from the days of Danish rule. Beside the fort are Emancipation Garden and Vendors' Plaza, where you can buy bags of inexpensive souvenirs. Farther west are restored Danish warehouses crisscrossed by cobblestoned shopping arcades, home to another cluster of boutiques and restaurants, as well as the major banks.

Play It Safe

USVI crime rates are high. Street smarts will go a long way toward ensuring a safe and relaxing vacation. Seek advice from your hotel concierge or the local tourist office before venturing into unfamiliar areas. Stick to well-lit, touristy areas at night, and don't hitchhike or accept rides from strangers. Don't leave valuables unattended, particularly at the beach. Use your hotel or cabin safe to secure wallets, passports and other important items.

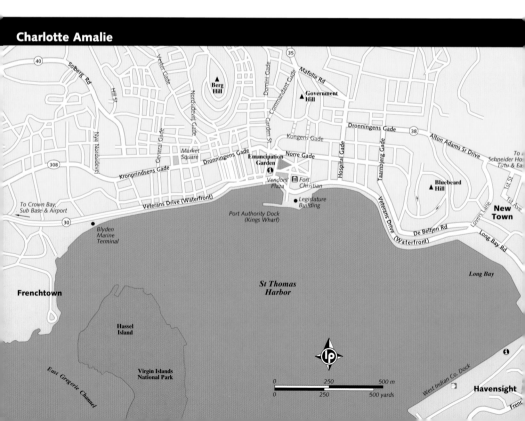

Charlotte Amalie

Departing from the marine terminal on Waterfront are ferries to St. John and seaplane connections to St. Croix and San Juan, Puerto Rico. At the west end of the bay is the Frenchtown neighborhood, known for its open-air fish market and restaurants. Farther west still is the Crown Bay cruise ship dock, then the airport.

Getting Around

For a quick orientation on any of the three main islands, hop aboard a safari bus—an open flatbed truck with covered seating. These independently operated trucks roam the main roads, making pickups along the way. Fares are typically only a few dollars each way. Taxi service is also available throughout the territory, using both mini vans and cars. Rates are published, but be sure to confirm your fare in advance. Another option is scheduled VITRAN bus service. Fares are $1, and the air-conditioning works most of the time.

You'll find both international and local car rental agencies in the major towns. Reserve a car well in advance if you plan to visit during high season. Four-wheel-drive vehicles are a popular option for back-road driving. Potholes and blind curves make travel by motorcycle, moped or bicycle dangerous. Charlotte Amalie

Island Driving Tips

First and foremost, remember to *keep left*. While cars here are left-hand drive (as on the mainland), driving in the USVI is on the left side of the road. This makes it difficult for drivers to see ahead when passing, so beware. A mandatory seatbelt law is strictly enforced.

Outside of the main towns, roads are not regularly maintained, with more potholes than pavement on some stretches, and no pavement at all on others. Roaming livestock is also a concern and can include anything from chickens and goats to cows, pigs and feral donkeys. Also be on the lookout for stray cats and dogs, whitetail deer, iguanas and mongooses.

Local drivers can be unpredictable, often stopping short to speak with friends or reversing their cars in the opposite lane of traffic. There is a common gesture drivers use in lieu of warning signals (no, not *that* gesture). When a driver is about to do something (stop, turn, whatever), he will extend his left arm out the window and waggle his hand vigorously up and down like a flapping bird— be prepared for *anything*!

often experiences heavy rush-hour traffic—factor that in when returning to your ship or making other plans.

Hitchhiking is widely practiced on St. John. That said, it's not advisable on any of the islands, as there have been reports of assaults on hitchhikers.

Regular passenger ferries operate between St. Thomas, St. John and the BVI. Terminals are located in Charlotte Amalie and Red Hook on St. Thomas and Cruz Bay on St. John. Car ferries and water taxis also operate between Red Hook and Cruz Bay. High-speed ferries connect St. Thomas and St. Croix, as do several commuter airlines, including the popular Seaborne seaplanes.

Entry

U.S. and Canadian citizens face no special requirements for entry, but must furnish proof of citizenship (a passport or a driver's license and birth certificate) for return to the mainland. Bring a passport if you plan a side trip to the neighboring BVIs.

Visitors from all other countries must have a valid passport. Some may need a visa. For more information contact the U.S. Immigration & Naturalization Service office on St. Thomas (☎ 774-4279, us-ins@usvi.net).

Time

The territory is on Atlantic Standard Time, one hour ahead of Eastern Standard Time. When it's noon in the USVI, it's 4pm in London, 11am in New York, 8am in San Francisco and 1am the following morning in Sydney. During daylight saving time, which is not observed in the Virgin Islands, the time is the same as EST.

Money

The U.S. dollar is the official currency throughout the U.S. and British Virgin Islands. Major credit cards are accepted at most hotels, restaurants, shops and car rental agencies. Traveler's checks are also widely accepted and offer greater protection from loss or theft. Personal checks are not accepted. ATMs are available at most banks and major shopping centers.

Restaurant waitstaff rely on tips for their livelihood. Tip 15 to 20% of the total bill, unless service is terrible. Some restaurants add the service charge. Tip taxi drivers and baggage carriers a dollar or two.

Electricity

As on the mainland, voltage in the USVI is 110V, 60 cycles, and plugs have two flat pins or three pins (two flat, one round). Three-pin plugs don't fit into two-hole sockets, but adapters are easy to find at department and hardware stores.

Tipping Your Divemaster

Divemasters are called upon to perform many tasks, from the most mundane, such as loading tanks and passing out cups of water, to the most critical—saving lives. Most dive opera-tors encourage divers to tip for good service. In the Virgin Islands, where the cost of living is very high, tips can substantially affect a divemaster's income and quality of life.

Most USVI dive op-erators recommend a standard tip of 15 to 20% of the dive bill. Nevertheless, tipping should not be automatic or considered obligatory. As in a restaurant, the tip should reflect your level of satisfaction. If you aren't happy with the service, tip less or not at all. Conversely, if you feel an extra effort was made, tip extra.

In most cases, tips are distributed equally among the crew, so you should hand your tip to the boat captain or to your divemaster. For teaching dives, instruc-tors should be tipped individually.

Though the islands may experience sporadic blackouts, most resorts are equipped with backup generators for uninterrupted service.

Weights & Measures

The USVI follows the imperial system of weights and measures. This book pro-vides both imperial and metric measurements, except for specific references in dive site descriptions, which are given in imperial units only. Please refer to the conversion chart on the inside back cover.

What to Bring

General

Pack light, comfortable clothing that offers protection from the intense tropical sun. Add a wide-brimmed hat, wraparound sunglasses and waterproof sunblock for full coverage. Casual dress is widely accepted, though traditional West Indian mores frown on short shorts, halter tops or swimsuits in town. Some restaurants may require dressier attire, so plan accordingly. If you plan any long hikes, pack appropriate footwear. Also bring plenty of insect repellent.

Dive-Related

Well-maintained rental gear is available at most dive centers, though you may want to bring your favorite mask and fins for the best fit. A lycra dive skin or 3mm shorty wetsuit is ample thermal protection in the summer, while a full 3mm suit will protect against coral scrapes and keep you toasty in winter. Consider bringing two bathing suits, so one will always be dry.

Underwater Photography

Warm, calm water and visibility that sometimes exceeds 100ft (30m) make the USVI an ideal place to practice underwater photography. Subjects include healthy reefs, colorful fish and interesting shipwrecks. Several dive shops rent underwater cameras, while some offer basic underwater photography courses. Most provide onboard freshwater rinse buckets for your camera and strobes.

Owning your own setup can be an expensive proposition. Consider taking advantage of the territory's duty-free status to purchase an underwater camera or other equipment. Try Boolchand's or Royal Caribbean in Charlotte Amalie.

Print film and batteries are widely available at supermarkets, drugstores, department stores and photo specialty stores, though slide film is harder to find. One-hour film processing is available throughout the territory.

Business Hours

Regular business hours are 8am to 5pm Monday to Friday. Shops stay open till about 8pm weekdays and Saturdays. Some offer limited Sunday hours. Found in the major towns, post offices are open 8am to 5pm weekdays and till noon Saturday. Banks are open 8:30am to 3pm Monday to Thursday and till 4pm Friday, with limited Saturday hours.

Accommodations

Accommodations in the USVI span all tastes and budgets, from luxury resorts to restored plantation greathouses, self-contained villas, guesthouses, small hotels and campgrounds. The territory recently legalized gambling, and a new resort-casino is now open on St. Croix. Camping is a favorite option, especially on St. John. Bare sites, eco-tents and rustic cabins are available at most campgrounds. Reservations are recommended at St. John's popular national park campgrounds.

High season, marked by good weather and high rates, runs from Dec. 15 to April 15. Low season runs from April 16 to Dec. 14, with lower rates but an increased risk of hurricanes. There is an 8% tax on all accommodations.

To narrow your search, contact the St. Croix Hotel Association (☎ 773-7117 or toll-free ☎ 800-524-2026, www.stcroixhotelandtourism.com) or the St. Thomas–St. John Hotel Association (☎ 774-6835, www.sttstjhta.com).

Dining & Food

Food vendors ply the tourist centers, and in a pinch there's always brand-name fast food. But more interesting alternatives exist. Breakfast options include resort buffets and several bakeries. Johnnycakes, made from fried or baked dough, are a popular morning treat. For lunch try any of several good delis or open-air cafés. Dinner choices range from casual hangouts to fancy restaurants with harbor views. You'll find West Indian, American, Italian, French, Greek, Chinese, Japanese, Thai and even fusion cuisine.

Local specialties include fresh seafood, especially mahimahi, wahoo and Caribbean spiny lobster (a sweeter clawless version of its Maine cousin). Other menu items you may find are roti (a meat-filled pastry—watch for bones), fungi (cornmeal boiled with okra) and callaloo (a creamy soup made with greens). Drink options include a variety of fresh fruit juices and mixed drinks made with local rum. Tap water is safe to drink at the resorts, and bottled water is widely available at markets and restaurants.

You'll find supermarkets, produce markets and roadside fruit stands on the main islands. Home-grown fruits include mangoes, papayas and genips (a grape-like fruit with a pit). A word to the wise: Don't confuse large brown plantains with bananas. Uncooked plantains taste like the paste you used in third grade—cooked, they're sweet and delicious.

Vendors will grill fresh seafood while you wait.

Shopping

Duty-free shopping is the magnet that draws cruise ships to the Virgin Islands. Big spenders flock here for the $1,200 per person duty-free allowance—triple that of other Caribbean islands. Bonus: There's no local sales tax. Sale items include jewelry, watches, cameras, electronics, arts and crafts, linens, clothing and liquor at soda pop prices.

Shoppers will find mecca at Havensight and Mountain Top malls and along Waterfront on St. Thomas, in Cruz Bay on St. John, and in Christiansted and Frederiksted on St. Croix. Comparison-shop for high-ticket items, and wait a vendor or two before snapping up souvenirs—you'll likely find a nicer T-shirt at a better price just around the corner.

For toiletries and other necessities, stop by the Kmart department stores on St. Thomas and St. Croix, with the same products as back home.

Duty-free bargains await visitors just steps from St. Thomas' West Indian Co. cruise ship dock.

Activities & Attractions

The Virgins are blessed with warm tropical waters that allow an array of watersports, from diving and snorkeling to board sailing and kayaking. Free spirits charter sleek sailboats, thrill-seekers try parasailing or skydiving and sports buffs choose tennis, golf or fishing. More grounded souls stroll through museums, historic ruins and botanical gardens. Shoppers surrender to duty-free bliss, while nature buffs find their paradise on powdery beaches and misty mountain trails.

Each island has unique draws. St. Thomas hosts the concerts and nightlife, while St. John promises respite for the weary. St. Croix offers more offbeat choices, from tours at the Cruzan Rum Distillery to the beer-swilling pigs at the Domino Club (ask a local about this one).

For more suggestions, contact the visitor information centers on all three islands (see Listings, page 124). If you're visiting during low season, call to confirm, as some places curtail hours or close altogether.

Virgin Islands National Park

St. John's charm lies in the rolling sweep of undeveloped hills within Virgin Islands National Park. Congress established the park in 1956 on land donated to the government by Laurance Rockefeller. Today the park embraces some three-fifths of St. John and includes Hassel Island in St. Thomas Harbor. More than 1 million annual visitors make this the territory's number one attraction.

Oft-photographed Trunk Bay, with its underwater snorkeling trail, anchors a series of spectacular beaches on the north shore. Just east are the Annaberg sugar mill ruins, overlooking Leinster Bay, a favorite snorkeling spot. Twenty-two maintained trails crisscross more than 20 miles of the island, taking in tropical forests, white-sand beaches, salt ponds, a Taino archaeological site, petroglyphs and plantation ruins. Park rangers lead two-hour hikes along the Reef Bay Trail, which ends at the beach for snorkeling and an easy boat ride back to town.

Camping is offered at Cinnamon Bay (☎ 800-539-9998, www.cinnamonbay.com). Reservations are required for all ranger-led activities. For more information call or visit the Cruz Bay Visitor Center (☎ 776-6201, www.nps.gov/viis) a short walk north of the ferry terminal.

St. John's celebrated Trunk Bay is a popular stop in Virgin Islands National Park.

A Day at the Beach

The territory boasts more than 100 beaches, all of which by law are open to the public. Though some are only accessible by boat, dozens more are only a short hike or safari bus ride away. Always ask permission before crossing private property. A few public beaches charge a nominal parking fee.

St. Thomas standouts include Magens Bay and Sapphire Beach. If you're seeking seclusion, take a tiny water taxi from Crown Bay Marina to reach Water Island's remote Honeymoon Beach. St. John claims about 40 white-sand stretches, from those at Caneel Bay resort to the national park favorites at Trunk, Cinnamon and Leinster Bays. Visitors to St. Croix should hop a boat to Buck Island or a cab to Cane Bay.

Nude sunbathing is against the law in the Virgin Islands. That said, those in search of an all-over tan take off for Little Magens Bay on St. Thomas, Isaac Bay on St. Croix, and St. John's Salomon Bay, a short hike west of the Caneel Bay property.

Sailing

Steady trade winds and hundreds of calm anchorages make this one of the easiest places to sail in the world. About a half dozen charter companies on St. Thomas and St. Croix offer both monohulls and catamarans. Certified sailors can bareboat charter their own vessel, while others can hire a captain and crew. Expect to pay about $5,000 per week in high season. Call the **Virgin Islands Charter Yacht League** for more information (toll-free ☎ 800-524-2061).

Those interested in learning to sail should contact **Annapolis Sailing School** in Christiansted (toll-free ☎ 800-638-9192, www.annapolissailing.com).

Aquariums

Adjacent to Coki Beach on St. Thomas' East End is **Coral World** marine park (☎ 775-1555 or toll-free ☎ 888-695-2073, www.coralworld.vi.com), where non-divers can get a first-hand look at a living reef. Perched 100ft (30m) offshore, a three-story observatory features undersea viewing ports, as well as a tank housing sharks, tarpon and barracuda. The park also offers turtle, stingray and baby shark pools, a touch pool, mangrove and aquarium exhibits, and an 80,000-gallon (300,000-liter) coral reef tank. For an extra charge, those wanting a closer look can try Sea Trekkin', a guided walk on the seafloor while wearing helmets fed by surface-supplied air. Bring a swimsuit and towel. Open daily 9am to 5pm.

In Christiansted, the **St. Croix Aquarium & Marine Education Center** (☎ 773-8995, www.geocities.com/stcroix-aquarium) is a 50-tank catch-and-release facility that houses between 100 and 300 species at any given time. Staff biologists lead half-hour tours, teaching visitors about marine life and environmental issues. High-season hours are 11am to 4pm Tuesday to Saturday.

Visitors to Coral World can try Sea Trekkin' in the shallows.

Seaborne Airlines

As beautiful as these islands are at sea level, nothing quite compares to a bird's eye view. Seaborne Airlines (☎ 773-6442 or toll-free ☎ 866-359-8784, www.seaborneairlines.com) offers pricey but unforgettable 45-minute "flightseeing" tours over St. Thomas, St. John and the BVI and similar 25-minute tours over St. Croix, with souvenir guidebooks and commentary on personal headphones. Its five deHavilland Twin-Otter seaplanes each seat between 15 and 19 passengers. Big picture windows make it easy to see and record all the sights. Flights leave from Seaborne's docks in Charlotte Amalie and Christiansted.

Atlantis Submarines

Atlantis (☎ 776-5650 or toll-free ☎ 800-253-0493, www.goatlantis.com/stthomas) offers a comfortable way to visit the underwater world with your nondiving friends. The company's 65ft (20m) air-conditioned submersible takes 46 passengers down to 80ft (24m) on a reef just south of St. Thomas. Gawk through big 2ft (60cm) portholes at brilliant corals, curious turtles and bewildered tropical fish, including the occasional reef shark. Bring a camera with high-speed film, but don't use a flash. The trip takes two hours, including a short boat ride to and from the waiting sub and nearly an hour underwater. The ticket office at Havensight Mall is open 8am to 5pm daily during high season and on weekdays during low season.

Nondiving visitors can view the reefs in comfort aboard Atlantis' air-conditioned submarine.

Estate Whim Plantation Museum

Two miles (3km) east of Frederiksted on Centerline Road (Route 70), Estate Whim features a largely restored 1800s sugar plantation, including three mills, slave quarters and a furnished greathouse with walls constructed of coral, limestone and rubble. Guided tours also take in art and historical exhibits, a furniture restoration shop and the cookhouse, with free johnnycake samples. The grounds are open Monday to Saturday 10am to 4pm (☎ 772-0598, www.stcroixlandmarks .org/whim.html).

St. George Village Botanical Garden

On Centerline Road (Route 70) a few miles east of Frederiksted, this 16-acre (6.5-hectare) botanical garden showcases more than 1,500 species of tropical plants. Over the centuries the grounds have hosted an Arawak Indian village, a

19th century Danish sugar plantation and a cattle ranch. Pick up a brochure at the reconstructed greathouse for a self-guided tour of the gardens and various ruins. Among other tidbits, you'll learn that the turpentine tree is nicknamed the tourist tree for its peeling red bark. Open daily 9am to 5pm (☎ 692-2874, www.sgvbg.com).

Kayaking

Several outfitters offer kayak tours through nearshore mangroves, as well as excursions to surrounding islands. Your guide will explain local ecology and point out resident marine life and birds. Both sit-on-top and seagoing kayaks are used, and basic instruction is often included. Wear your swimsuit and a wide-brimmed hat and bring sunblock, a towel and a waterproof camera.

On St. Thomas' East End, **Virgin Islands Ecotours** (☎ 779-2155, jwbc-pastt@att.net) offers a 2.5-hour guided tour of the Mangrove Lagoon Marine Sanctuary, including a 45-minute stop for snorkeling. St. John's **Arawak Expeditions** (☎ 693-8312 or toll-free ☎ 800-238-8687; www.arawakexp.com) operates sea kayak daytrips from Cruz Bay to the Pillsbury Sound cays, as well as five-day excursions to the neighboring BVI. **Caribbean Adventure Tours** (☎ 773-4599, www.tourcarib.com) visits St. Croix's Salt River Bay Ecological Preserve and offers sunset and moonlight paddles. Based at Cane Bay, **Virgin Kayak Co.** (☎ 778-0071, www.virginkayak.com) tours St. Croix's north shore.

Don't Stop the Carnival!

In the Virgin Islands, Carnival is a no-holds-barred celebration of West Indian culture. The modern-day version was initiated on St. Thomas in 1952, and the island still kicks things off in April with the territory's biggest party. Month-long festivities feature an early-morning band tramp, dance band and calypso competitions, beauty pageants, a food festival, games and rides. The party wraps up

with colorful, raucous, slow-moving parades—one for children, the other decidedly adult. Both feature traditional mocko jumbies (costumed stilt walkers who represent spirits, or jumbies, in African lore). During the adult parade, you can't help but notice couples "workin' up" (working up a sweat) in gyrating, bump-and-grind dances.

St. John's smaller-scale Carnival celebration coincides with the July Fourth holiday, while St. Croix waits till December to hold its Crucian Christmas Festival.

Whale Watching

The **Environmental Association of St. Thomas–St. John** (EAST; ☎ 776-1976, www.usvi.net/east) sponsors whale-watching trips in February and March, when humpbacks migrate through these waters with newborn calves in tow. The boat

cruises into deep water north of the islands while a spotter plane directs them toward surfacing whale pods. But don't expect close encounters. Nursing humpbacks are naturally wary of human contact, and the Marine Mammal Protection Act forbids boats from approaching within 100 yards of the whales. Still, at 45 to 50ft (14 to 15m) long and weighing 25 to 30 tons (23 to 27 metric tons), adult humpbacks are hard to miss. You'll see them spout and occasionally "spy-hop" to have a look around. If you're lucky, you may even see one breach, a sight that inspires spontaneous cheers from onlookers.

Breaching humpbacks are an unforgettable sight.

Horseback Riding

Stables on St. Croix and St. John offer two- to four-hour rides along hillside trails and sandy beaches. Call in advance for age and weight restrictions.

Just north of Frederiksted, **Paul and Jill's Equestrian Stables** (☎ 772-2880 or ☎ 772-2627, www.paulandjills.com) offers daily rides through the tropical forest. In St. John's Coral Bay, **Carolina Corral** (☎ 693-5778) offers trail rides by horse or donkey.

Golfing

Duffers will be as pleased as divers with the USVI. St. Thomas boasts the Tom and George Fazio–designed par-70 **Mahogany Run Golf Course** (☎ 777-6006 or toll-free ☎ 800-253-7103, www.st-thomas.com/mahogany). St. Croix offers three courses: the Robert Trent Jones–designed par-72 **Carambola Golf Club** (☎ 778-5638, www.carambolagolf.com); the Bob Joyce–designed par-70 course at the **Buccaneer Hotel** (☎ 712-2100 or toll-free ☎ 800-255-3881, www.thebuccaneer.com /golf.htm); and a nine-hole course at **The Reef** (☎ 773-8844).

Diving Health & Safety

The USVI is a generally healthy travel destination and poses no serious health risks to most visitors. For most foreign visitors, no immunizations are required for entry. Adequate medical attention is available on all three islands, although valid health or travel insurance is advisable, as medical costs can be quite high. You'll find well-stocked pharmacies in the major towns.

The tropical sun should be your primary concern. Children and snorkelers are particularly vulnerable to sunburn. Stay out of the sun between 10am and 2pm, when the sun's rays are most intense, and be especially wary on hazy days, when the rays are deceptively strong. Use a waterproof sunblock with high sun protection factor (SPF), and reapply it frequently, especially after being in the water. Wear a hat and polarized sunglasses and keep to the shade whenever possible. Treat sunburn seriously, and immediately seek medical attention if there's blistering or signs of infection. When planning a long hike, be sure to bring plenty of bottled drinking water.

Diving & Flying

Many divers in the Virgin Islands arrive by plane. While it's fine to dive soon *after* flying, it's important to remember that your last dive should be completed at least 24 hours *before* your flight to minimize the risk of decompression sickness, caused by residual nitrogen in the blood.

While you'll do more deep diving along the walls north of St. Croix, the territory's only recompression chamber is on St. Thomas, a 20-minute flight north. When flying between the islands, if you suspect decompression sickness or simply want to avoid the risk of DCS, instruct your pilot to stay below 500ft (150m).

The other main concern is dengue fever, which has reached epidemic proportions in the region in recent years. This mosquito-borne disease causes fever accompanied by an itchy rash and severe muscle and joint pain that can last for several days. Serious complications are rare. There is no treatment for the disease, though hospitals can address your symptoms. Your best defense against dengue is to avoid mosquito bites. Use insect repellent liberally and avoid the beaches at dawn and dusk when biting insects are most active.

Pre-Trip Preparation

Your general state of health, diving skill level and specific equipment needs are the three most important factors that impact any dive trip. If you honestly assess these before you leave, you'll be well on your way to assuring a safe dive trip.

Tips for Evaluating a Dive Boat

In the USVI dive boats range from small motor vessels for up to six passengers (known as six-packs) to large pontoon boats that can accommodate several dozen divers. Most boats are U.S. Coast Guard inspected and adhere to strict operating standards. Licensed boats must have two-way radios and carry enough life jackets for each passenger aboard. Captains must remain aboard at all times. A well-equipped dive boat also carries oxygen, a diver recall device and a first-aid kit. Larger boats often have a shaded area and a supply of fresh drinking water. Some provide a freshwater shower and a marine toilet. On night dives, a good boat will have powerful lights, including a strobe light.

Your crew should give a thorough pre-dive briefing that explains procedures for dealing with an emergency when divers are in the water. The crew should also explain how divers enter the water and get back onboard. If there is a strong current, they should deploy a weighted descent line and a drift line from the stern. For deep dives the crew should hang a safety tank at 15ft (5m). When carrying groups, a good crew will get everyone's name on the dive roster so that it can initiate an immediate search if a diver is missing. This is something you should always verify.

First, if you're not in shape, start exercising. Second, if you haven't dived for a while (six months is too long) and your skills are rusty, do a local dive with an experienced buddy or take a scuba review course. Feeling good physically and diving regularly will make you a safer diver and enhance your enjoyment underwater.

At least a month before your trip, inspect your dive gear. Remember, your regulator should be serviced annually, whether you've used it or not. If you use a dive computer and can replace the battery yourself, change it before the trip or buy a spare one to take along. Otherwise, send the computer to the manufacturer for a battery replacement.

If possible, find out if the dive center rents or services the type of gear you own. If not, you might want to take spare parts or even spare gear. An extra mask is always a good idea.

Purchase any additional equipment you might need, such as a dive light and tank marker light for night diving, a line reel for wreck diving, etc. Make sure you have at least a whistle attached to your BC. Better yet, add a marker tube (also known as a safety sausage or come-to-me).

About a week before taking off, do a final check of your gear, grease o-rings, check batteries and assemble a save-a-dive kit. This kit should at minimum contain extra mask and fin straps, snorkel keeper, mouthpiece, valve cap, zip ties and o-rings.

DAN

Divers Alert Network (DAN) is an international membership association of individuals and organizations sharing a common interest in diving and safety. It operates a 24-hour diving emergency hotline in the U.S.: ☎ **919-684-8111 or 919-684-4DAN** (-4326). The latter accepts collect calls in a dive emergency. Though DAN does not directly provide medical care, it does provide advice on early treatment, evacuation and hyperbaric treatment of diving-related injuries. Divers should contact DAN for assistance as soon as a diving emergency is suspected.

DAN membership is reasonably priced and includes DAN TravelAssist, a benefit that covers medical air evacuation from anywhere in the world for any illness or injury. For a small additional fee, divers can get secondary insurance coverage for decompression illness. For membership details, contact DAN at ☎ 800-446-2671 in the U.S. or ☎ 919-684-2948 elsewhere. DAN can also be reached at www.diversalertnetwork.com.

Medical & Recompression Facilities

Compared to the rest of the Caribbean, infrastructure and services in the Virgin Islands are pretty good. That said, they often fall short of stateside standards. Nowhere is this more critical than with medical care. Hospitals have struggled in the past to meet accreditation standards, and emergency service vehicles are poorly maintained.

There is, however, a capably staffed recompression chamber on St. Thomas. The key is getting the patient to the chamber quickly. Check in advance whether your dive operator has a backup plan in case the ambulance can't make it. If DCS is suspected, the patient should be kept on pure oxygen while en route to the hospital. If a diving accident occurs on St. Croix, arrangements should be made to airlift the patient to the chamber on St. Thomas or to better-equipped hospitals in Puerto Rico or Miami.

Medical Contacts

Emergency medical services (medical, police, fire) ☎ 911

U.S. Coast Guard Search & Rescue (VHF Channel 16) ☎ 787-289-2040

St. Thomas	St. John	St. Croix
Roy L. Schneider Hospital ☎ 776-8311	**Myrah Keating Smith Community Health Center** ☎ 693-8900	**Gov. Juan F. Luis Hospital** ☎ 778-6311
Recompression chamber ☎ 776-2686	**Morris de Castro Clinic** ☎ 776-6400	
Dr. David Boaz (dive medicine specialist) ☎ 774-8998		

Diving the U.S. Virgin Islands

As the USVI is divided by geography, so the diving also varies between north and south. St. Thomas and St. John feature healthy fringing reefs atop the shallow Virgin Bank. Maximum depths on the reefs average less than 60ft (18m), while the deepest wrecks just south of St. Thomas lie at about 100ft (30m). Forty miles (64km) to the south, St. Croix is perched atop its own narrow bank. The island's north shore borders the abyssal Virgin Trough, with slopes and sheer walls that plunge well below the sport-diving limit of 130ft (40m). Just outside Christiansted, Buck Island's barrier reef shelters a shallow lagoon, while the West End's calm waters harbor several wrecks and the Frederiksted Pier.

More than 500 fish species, 40 types of coral and hundreds of invertebrates thrive on the Virgin reefs. You'll find dozens of colorful reef fish in the shallows, darting amid healthy fringing reefs and atop steep reef buttresses. Mornings are the best times for sighting skittish Caribbean and blacktip reef sharks, while the night welcomes prowling octopuses to the open reef. Three of the world's seven sea turtle species inhabit these waters. The luckiest divers may catch sight of a dolphin or be serenaded by a humpback whale.

Diving Conditions

Welling up through the Lesser Antilles, the North Equatorial Current washes the Virgin Islands with warm, clear seas. Visibility averages between 60 and 70ft (18 and 21m), though it sometimes exceeds 100ft (30m). Water temperatures mirror the air temperature, dipping to about 76°F (24°C) in the winter and rising to about 86°F (30°C) in summer. Divers seldom need anything thicker than a 3mm shorty wetsuit.

The wind and waves often dictate where you'll dive. In winter months, cold fronts from the north bring strong swells and "Christmas winds" (sustained blows of 25 to 30 knots) to the Virgins' north shores, and diving shifts to the lee shores and protected coves. Ten- to 15-knot easterly trade winds in spring offer ideal diving and sailing conditions, with waves generally no higher than 3ft (1m). The winds gradually swing down out of the southeast by summer, the best time to dive the north shores. Unsettled conditions herald the onset of hurricane season, which runs from June through November.

While generally unnoticeable, tidal currents do rip through the narrows between islands. Be sure someone aboard is watching your bubbles and is prepared to pick you up.

Dive operators offer at least three dives a day—typically a two-tank dive in the morning, followed by a one- or two-tank dive in the afternoon. Most also offer night dives and special trips, such as dives to witness coral spawning, whale-watching cruises and daytrips to the neighboring British Virgin Islands. Some are affiliated with adjacent resorts and can offer discounted diving/accommodation packages. Most operate dive vessels, though some are shore-based and boast specialized knowledge of the nearshore reefs. Several offer nitrox for qualified divers. (See Listings, pages 119-123, for contact details.)

Each shop specializes in a particular region and typically visits sites within 20 or 30 minutes of the dock, affording divers plenty of time to explore the reefs and wrecks. While only a handful of dive operators offer dedicated snorkeling excursions, there are many daytrip boats that will take groups out for a day of sightseeing, snorkeling and lunch aboard. Check with your hotel concierge or cruise operator for more information.

Dive Training & Certification

The USVI is an excellent place to begin or continue your dive training. Most dive operators teach a full range of courses, from basic Open Water through Divemaster and specialties such as wreck diving, deep diving and underwater photography. If you haven't been diving in a while, you may want to take a scuba refresher course.

Offering clear, calm waters, the USVI is an ideal spot to start or further your dive education.

Those interested in trying scuba for the first time can enroll in a resort course. This one-day program begins with a classroom session on basic diving theory, followed by practice on scuba gear in a pool, then a guided open-water dive.

If you already plan to be certified but don't want to spend your vacation in a classroom, consider a referral program. You'll enroll in classroom and pool sessions at a dive center near your home, then complete your open-water dives with a dive center in the USVI.

Snuba

Snuba offers would-be divers an introduction to scuba in water no deeper than 20ft (6m). Participants wear a mask, fins, weight belt and light harness, which holds a standard scuba regulator. An air hose connects the regulator to a tank that floats in an inflatable raft at the surface. Divers are free to swim about, towing the raft behind them.

V.I. Snuba Excursions (693-8063; www.visnuba.com) conducts 30- to 40-minute guided underwater tours at Trunk Bay on St. John and Coki Beach on St. Thomas. Tours at Coki Beach include complimentary passes to Coral World marine park. Anyone age 8 or older and in good health may participate. Reservations are recommended.

Snorkeling

Warm, clear water and generally calm conditions make snorkeling here a popular pastime. Floating gently only a few yards above the reef, you'll see healthy corals, dozens of fish, sleek rays and the occasional turtle or octopus.

A few simple precautions will guarantee a safe and rewarding glimpse at life beneath the waves. First, seek advice from local dive shops about snor-

The Virgins' Top Snorkeling Spots

Following are a few of the better-known snorkeling spots in the USVI. There are dozens more throughout the islands. Ask local dive operators and national park rangers for more suggestions. Dive shops and charter companies on St. Thomas and St. John also offer snorkeling daytrips to the neighboring British Virgin Islands, featuring Jost Van Dyke, the caves at Norman Island and The Baths on Virgin Gorda.

St. Thomas	St. John	St. Croix
Coki Beach	Haulover Bay	Buck Island
Hull Bay	Leinster Bay	Cane Bay
Sapphire Beach	Salt Pond Bay	Cramer Park
Secret Harbor	Trunk Bay	

Snorkelers can choose from among dozens of secluded anchorages and nearshore reefs.

keling conditions. Chances are they'll know the best sites, the easiest entry and exit points and the existence of any hazards such as sea urchin colonies or strong currents.

Wait till you're in waist-deep water to don and doff your fins (it's much easier to walk on sand than to waddle like a duck). Also wet and pull back your hair before putting on your mask, and check for any leaks before heading for deeper water.

If caught in a strong current, don't try to swim against it—you'll exhaust yourself. Instead, signal someone ashore and swim with the current to a safe exit point farther down shore. Consider the walk back a free lesson in humility.

Finally, respect the tropical sun. Always apply waterproof sunblock to your ears, neck, back and the back of your legs—any exposed skin that will be "sunny side up" as you snorkel. Many snorkelers wear an old T-shirt or lycra dive skin for added coverage.

Dive Site Icons

The symbols at the beginning of each dive site description provide a quick summary of some of the following characteristics present at each site:

 Good snorkeling or free-diving site.

 Remains or partial remains of a wreck can be seen at this site.

 Sheer wall or drop-off.

 Deep dive. Features of this dive occur in water deeper than 90ft (27m).

 Strong currents may be encountered at this site.

 Strong surge (the horizontal movement of water caused by waves) may be encountered at this site.

 Drift dive. Because of strong currents and/or difficulty in anchoring, a drift dive is recommended at this site.

 Beach/shore dive. This site can be accessed from shore.

 Poor visibility. The site often has visibility of less than 40ft (12m).

 Caves are a prominent feature of this site. Only experienced cave divers should explore inner cave areas.

 Marine preserve. Special regulations apply in this area.

Pisces Rating System for Dives & Divers

The dive sites in this book are rated according to the following diver skill-level rating system. These are not absolute ratings but apply to divers at a particular time, diving at a particular place. For instance, someone unfamiliar with prevailing conditions might be considered a novice diver at one dive area, but an intermediate diver at another, more familiar location.

Novice: A novice diver should be accompanied by an instructor, divemaster or advanced diver on all dives. A novice diver generally fits the following profile:

◆ basic scuba certification from an internationally recognized certifying agency
◆ dives infrequently (less than one trip a year)
◆ logged fewer than 25 total dives
◆ little or no experience diving in similar waters and conditions
◆ dives no deeper than 60ft (18m)

Intermediate: An intermediate diver generally fits the following profile:

◆ may have participated in some form of continuing diver education
◆ logged between 25 and 100 dives
◆ dives no deeper than 130ft (40m)
◆ has been diving in similar waters and conditions within the last six months

Advanced: An advanced diver generally fits the following profile:

◆ advanced certification
◆ has been diving for more than two years and logged over 100 dives
◆ has been diving in similar waters and conditions within the last six months

Regardless of your skill level, you should be in good physical condition and know your limitations. If you are uncertain of your own level of expertise for a particular site, ask the advice of a local dive instructor. He or she is best qualified to assess your abilities based on the site's prevailing dive conditions. Ultimately, however, you must decide if you are capable of making a particular dive, a decision that should take into account your level of training, recent experience and physical condition, as well as the conditions at the site. Remember that conditions can change at any time, even during a dive.

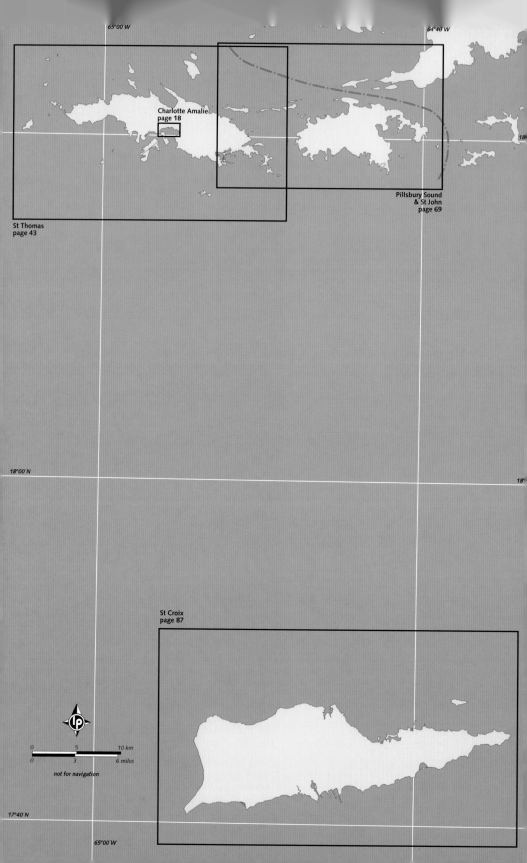

65°00' W

64°40' W

18°

Charlotte Amalie
page 18

Pillsbury Sound
& St John
page 69

St Thomas
page 43

18°00' N

18°

St Croix
page 87

0   5   10 km
0   3   6 miles

not for navigation

17°40' N

65°00' W

St. Thomas & St. John Dive Sites

These sister islands are linked by a thin ribbon of cays that stretch 6 miles (10km) across Pillsbury Sound. Dive operators out of St. Thomas' East End and St. John's West End regularly visit several dozen sites in and around the sound. The cays' windward north shores offer fascinating caves, arches, tunnels and sheer walls. When the weather turns rough, diving shifts to sheltered fringing reefs within the sound. Travel times average about 10 to 20 minutes from either island.

St. Thomas boasts the better-developed dive industry. Nearly a dozen dive shops are spread out from Lindbergh Bay near the airport around the East End to Coki Beach. Diving largely centers on scattered shipwrecks and rocky islands fanned out along the south shore. Most sites are within 20 minutes of the dock, though there are several advanced sites on outlying rocks to the north and south.

In addition to the Pillsbury Sound sites, dive operators on St. John visit a series of fringing reefs in protected waters along the south shore. There's another concentration of sites around Coral Bay on the East End, home to just one dive operator. Just south of the bay is Eagle Shoal, a rocky maze that has hosted several underwater weddings.

If weather thwarts diving at your chosen site, don't despair—your dive operator knows dozens of sites in addition to those that follow.

DAVID LAUTERBORN

These neighboring islands are watersports havens.

41

St. Thomas

About the size of Manhattan, St. Thomas is the USVI government seat, main arrival point, tourism hub and unabashed salesman. If the island is the heart of the territory, then Charlotte Amalie provides the pulse. The town sprawls over the hills surrounding St. Thomas Harbor, a wide crescent at the center of the south shore. This is where you'll find the restaurants, clubs and duty-free shops. Crowds

St. Thomas Dive Sites

	Good Snorkeling	Novice	Intermediate	Advanced
1 Rough Point				●
2 The Arena				●
3 Creaking Rock			●	
4 *Miss Opportunity*			●	
5 *Witshoal II*			●	
6 *Witservice IV*			●	
7 Blackbeard's Eye & The Fence			●	
8 Grain Wreck (*Grainton*)			●	
9 *Witconcrete II*			●	
10 Sprat Point		●		
11 Kennedy Wreck		●		
12 Navy Barges		●		
13 Armando's Paradise		●		
14 *Cartanza Señora* & Buck Island Cove	●	●		
15 André's Reef & Dive Flag Rock		●		
16 Submarine Alley (Snapper Valley)			●	
17 Joe's Jam (Coral Bowl)		●		
18 Frenchman's Cap (Frenchcap Cay)			●	
19 Cow & Calf		●		
20 Ledges of Little St. James		●		
21 Coki Beach	●	●		

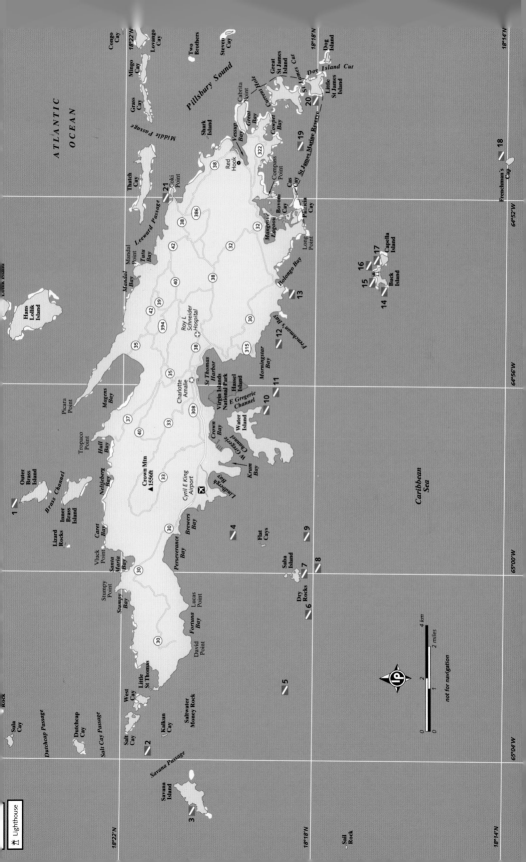

of pink-skinned tourists mingle with uniformed West Indian schoolchildren, and traffic jams regularly clog the streets with taxis, safari buses and gleaming cars that vibrate with throbbing Reggae, dub and Calypso.

Two small islands shield the harbor from the open sea. Known as the "fourth Virgin," Water Island is home to some 125 residents who know each other by name. Closer to shore is Hassel Island, its 120 acres (50 hectares) a satellite of Virgin Islands National Park on St. John.

Wrapping around the East End is a stretch of sandy beaches backed by upscale resorts. In their midst is Red Hook, the sportfishing center and gateway to St. John. Passenger and car ferries leave every half hour for Cruz Bay, 20 minutes east across Pillsbury Sound. Other attractions include the resort beach at Sapphire and Coki Beach, home to Coral World marine park.

Safari buses visit a scattering of touristy overlooks, including the harbor view from Paradise Point and views of mile-long Magens Bay from Drake's Seat and Mountain Top, self-proclaimed "birthplace of the banana daiquiri." Locals seeking refuge head to the wide beaches and rolling hills of the North Side, anchored by 1,556ft (467m) Crown Mountain.

1 Rough Point

Off the exposed North Side, Outer Brass boasts a steep shoreline of uplifted limestone slabs that tilt at all angles. The rock formations continue underwater at this site, forming pinnacles, sheer walls, caves and tunnels. Wait for flat seas before even considering a dive here. Winter swells often rule out a visit.

Dive operators anchor in 75ft just west of the point, where a series of three

Location: North tip of Outer Brass Island

Depth Range: Surface-90ft (27m)

Access: Boat

Expertise Rating: Advanced

or four fat pinnacles rise toward the surface from 90ft. Clouds of silversides shroud the peaks, attracting tarpon and barracuda. The first divers down often spot reef sharks.

Keep the pinnacles to your right as you follow schooling snappers and jacks over a jumble of boulders into a pebble-strewn, V-shaped channel. This channel leads up into "The Magazine," a vast sea cave whose walls meet

Near the rocky point, a sea cave delves underwater.

above water. As you ascend into darkness, the walls narrow to a flat tunnel at 30ft. Copper sweepers patrol its entrance. Do not enter if there's any surge. The tunnel runs back another 50ft, narrows, then shoots straight up to an air pocket at 20ft—keep your regulator in, as the stale air is unsafe to breathe.

Throughout the site you'll find pairs of banded and foureye butterflyfish, queen and French angels, rock beauties, trumpetfish, chromis and creole wrasses amid sponges and gorgonians. Return up and over the pinnacles, then through blue water for your safety stop beneath the boat.

What Are Gorgonians?

The term *gorgonians* refers to a group of corals that includes sea fans, sea plumes, sea whips and sea rods. Unlike hard corals, gorgonians have a flexible skeleton that sways in the water. This, combined with a common branching structure, gives them the appearance of plants. They are animals, however, colonies of coral polyps that extend into the current to feed on microscopic organisms. The branches also shelter a number of other marine creatures, including small fish, crabs and snails, as well as basket and brittle stars.

2 The Arena

This jumble of volcanic rock juts up sharply from blue water to within 25ft of the surface. At its peak, the massive slabs form a loose ring around a gorgonian-laden bowl, hence the name. Strong currents make this an advanced dive. If you miss the peak, you'll end up riding the current into open ocean with depths below 100ft. Plan your dive for slack tide.

The boulders form deep slots, canyons, undercuts and mini walls. Watch what you touch, as fire coral coats many surfaces. The sandy bowl is carpeted in sea rods, sea plumes and deepwater sea fans

Location: Savana Passage, NW of Kalkun Cay

Depth Range: 25-70ft+ (8-21m+)

Access: Boat

Expertise Rating: Advanced

amid several sponge species, notably azure vase, giant barrel and blue-gray branching vase. Protected recesses shelter cup corals and palm-sized pink *Stylaster* hydrocorals.

Blue tangs, creole wrasses, brown chromis, harlequin bass and pairs of banded and four-eye butterflyfish flit atop the gorgonians beside such larger specimens as queen triggerfish, Spanish hogfish, porkfish, rock beauties, gray angelfish and orangespotted filefish. Check reef nooks for spiny and slipper lobsters, squirrelfish and glass-eye snappers. The undercuts are a known resting place for nurse sharks. Watch the blue water for passing yellowtail snappers, bar jacks, southern sennets and bigger pelagics.

Deepwater sea fans thrive at this current-swept site.

3 Creaking Rock

In a protected cove off rocky Savana Island, this site is named for a large sub-merged boulder that rocks and creaks audibly in the surge like an old wooden ship. Boats moor on a boulder-strewn seafloor at about 50ft. The most dramatic formations are on the southwest end of the cove and continue around the point. Currents can be strong at the point, so be sure someone aboard is watching your bubbles.

Location: NW side of Savana Island

Depth Range: Surface-65ft (20m)

Access: Boat

Expertise Rating: Intermediate

The bottom is covered in a mix of corals amid branching vase sponges, sea rods and sea fans. The real attraction, however, is the topography, featuring sheer-walled galleries, deep undercuts and a series of pinnacles at the point that climb from 65ft to break the sur-face. Their current-swept faces are painted in encrusting sponges and flow-ery cup corals.

You'll find marine life in all shapes and sizes, from spider-like arrow crabs to large solitary snappers. Common reef fish include tangs, damselfish, mixed chromis, fairy basslets, queen and gray angels, rock beauties and pairs of four-eye, spotfin and banded butterflyfish. You'll also spot such gems as smooth trunkfish, spotted drums and the slender, cigarette-sized pipefish, a relative of the seahorse. The latter rely on camouflage for survival, so resist the temptation to pick them up.

The reef nooks shelter large lobsters, hinds, squirrelfish and glasseye snappers. Glance up to spot yellowtail snappers, bar jacks and barracuda shadowed by opportunistic scad.

4 *Miss Opportunity*

In her twilight years this WWII Navy hospital barge was docked off Sub Base and used as government office space. Sunk as an artificial reef in the mid-1980s, she came to rest upside down on the sand at 90ft. More than 300ft long, the ship lists to starboard, her port side facing the surface. It's easy to get disoriented inside the wreck. Note the nearest exits, and watch your air supply.

Boats anchor to the wreck, and divers descend the line to the upturned hull, which tops out at 55ft. Her double decks are an impressive sight, with open hatches, windows and rails that run the length of the ship. You'll enter a large hole at the stern. Windows and hatches allow plenty of natural light, so a dive light is optional, though you should avoid kicking up the thick layers of silt.

You'll first reach the surgery chamber, with intact light fixtures and what's thought to be an operating table. Remember, the floor is up and the ceiling is down. Weave single file through following rooms and passageways, keeping an eye out for pipes, air ducts and debris such as stacked tires. Branching tube sponges also sprout here and there.

You'll exit at the bow, where rails are wreathed in bushy white octocorals. Allow time to visit the keel, which is carpeted in encrusting corals and a forest of rope sponges. Colonies

Location: Just south of airport runway

Depth Range: 55-90ft (17-27m)

Access: Boat

Expertise Rating: Intermediate

of feathery hydroids add a delicate touch. Look beneath the twin fins astern to find a field of orange cup corals.

Mixed snappers and grunts move about the wreck, along with Spanish hogfish, parrotfish, blue tangs and sergeant majors. The first divers down often meet the stout resident goliath grouper, or jewfish. A careful observer will spot fire worms crawling along the hull—hands off, as their soft-looking hairy tufts will break off in your skin and feel like a severe burn.

Encrusting life coats the hull and rails of this former hospital barge.

5 *Witshoal II*

Local divers' favorite wreck, this time-worn West Indies Transport Co. freighter was sunk here in 1985 and has become a canvas for colorful encrusting life. The former tank landing ship (see sidebar) has an overall length of 327ft, 9 inches, with a 50ft beam. She lies in 90ft of water, her pilothouse topping out at

Location: Just west of Saba Island

Depth Range: 30-90ft (9-27m)

Access: Boat

Expertise Rating: Intermediate

about 30ft. Strong currents whip up in the channel, often dictating whether a second dive is possible. Operators tie to the wreck and use the line for descents and ascents.

The hull is a thriving artificial reef, boasting a thick coat of cup corals and encrusting sponges. Deepwater sea fans and white telesto octocorals grow in the shadows. Mixed schools of yellowtail snappers, creole wrasses, brown chromis and silvery blue boga swirl over the decks, while bar and horse-eye jacks

Orange cup corals coat the open stern deck.

Large Slow Target

Built by the Kaiser Co. shipyard in Vancouver, Washington, the *Witshoal II* was launched in 1943 as a Navy LST, or tank landing ship. During WWII, 1,051 of these ships were built. Each could carry up to 20 Sherman tanks, railroad cars, combat vehicles, equipment and troops in an amphibious assault. The ships were fitted with bow doors that would swing open to deploy a 112ft (34m) hydraulic launch ramp onto a beachhead. The welded seams of such doors are still visible on the bow of the *Witshoal II*. Just behind the wheelhouse are two anti-aircraft gun turrets, as well as ventilation shafts that once led down to the tank deck.

Tank landing ships were used during the allied invasion of Europe and the island-hopping campaigns of the South Pacific. With a cruising speed of less than 9 knots, LSTs were nicknamed "large slow targets," though fewer than 30 were lost in action during the war. The *Witshoal II*'s LST number and war record remain a mystery.

After the war, the ship was decommissioned, sold and converted into a cargo ship in 1952. Over her 32-year postwar career she hauled wood pulp on the Great Lakes as the *Frank J. Humphrey* and ferried liner board and bulk cargo from the East Coast to the West Indies as the *Witshoal II*. The freighter was moored in Krum Bay when Tropical Storm Klaus rolled through in early November 1984, sinking the ship. Her owners refloated the freighter, salvaged what they could, then towed her out toward Saba Island and sank her in late May 1985.

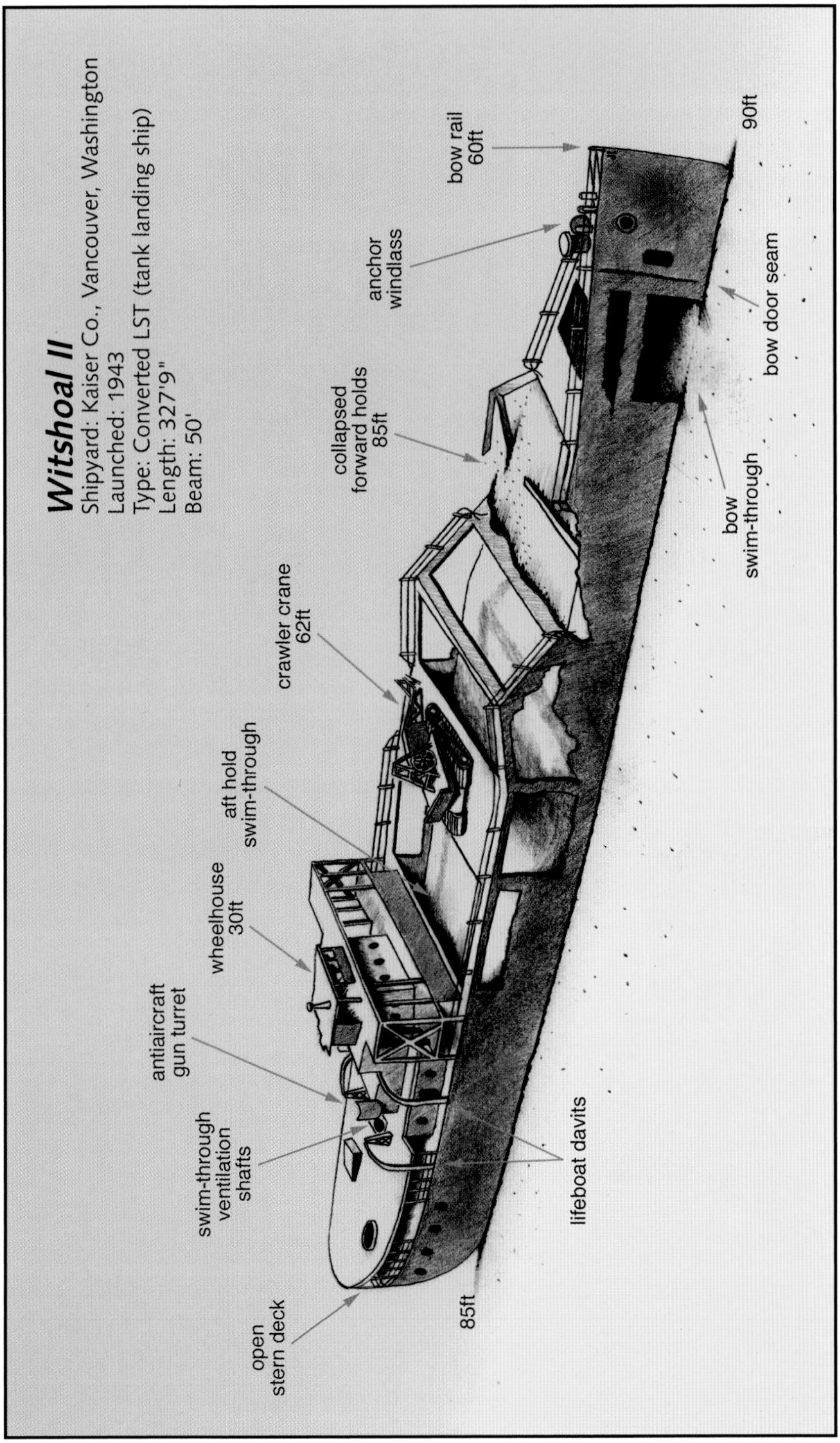

Witshoal II

Shipyard: Kaiser Co., Vancouver, Washington
Launched: 1943
Type: Converted LST (tank landing ship)
Length: 327'9"
Beam: 50'

bow rail
60ft

90ft

anchor
windlass

bow door seam

collapsed
forward holds
85ft

bow
swim-through

crawler crane
62ft

aft hold
swim-through

wheelhouse
30ft

antiaircraft
gun turret

swim-through
ventilation
shafts

lifeboat davits

85ft

open
stern deck

DAVID LAUTERBORN

patrol the perimeter. Groupers and barracuda frequent the wheelhouse. Large rays and blacktip sharks make an occasional appearance.

Tours often start at the bow, where the forward holds buckled when she sank. If you're lucky, you may spot a resident grouper the size of a steamer trunk. Swim up over the holds toward the superstructure. Resist the temptation to pull yourself along, as fire coral and stinging hydroids coat many surfaces. Amidships,

As you tour the superstructure, expect to meet one or perhaps both large resident barracuda.

an industrial crane sits on the deck, its long arm broken—one half on deck and the other in the sand below. Behind it is the aft hold, with access to an enclosed stern deck and down to the engine room.

To exit the hold, return the way you came or penetrate deeper and emerge through holes on either side of the ship's propellers. You may also ascend one at a time through one of two narrow ventilation shafts at the rear of the hold—not for the faint of heart or thick of waist. Spend the rest of your dive exploring the hallways, wheelhouse and open stern deck, which is coated in orange cup corals and home to a pair of large barracuda.

6 Witservice IV

This coastal tug was brought down from the cold waters off Maine. On April Fool's Day 1979, the *Witservice IV* was towing a barge along the south side when she struck the nearby Dry Rocks, popping rivets on her hull. Taking on water, she drifted with the current. Her crew fled to the barge, cut the tug loose and watched her sink. Blue Island Divers rediscovered the wreck in 2001. As she lies in open water, currents dictate if and when a dive is possible.

Lying on her port side atop sand at 100ft, the 123ft tug is remarkably intact, with her original rudder and prop, engine, winches, ropes and lines, gauges and brass portholes with glass panes. The only signs of age are her collapsed funnel and wheelhouse.

Divers make their way down the anchor line, first reaching the starboard

Location: Southwest of Saba Island

Depth Range: 80-100ft (24-30m)

Access: Boat

Expertise Rating: Intermediate

rail at 80ft. The hull is painted in encrusting sponges and corals, including delicate cup corals. You'll also find stands of rope and branching tube sponges in several colors. Watch for fire coral and feathery stinging hydroids.

Brown chromis, blue tangs and sergeant majors sweep the deck for algae, while Atlantic spadefish and bar jacks cruise the perimeter. Check holes along the starboard keel for squirrelfish, large snappers and resting hawksbill turtles. Deck openings beneath the superstructure allow a look inside, and advanced divers may penetrate all the way to the stern, home to a 5ft goliath grouper, or jewfish.

About 500ft astern of the tug lies the barge *Mist*, a large converted military ship that was sunk here shortly after the sinking of the *Witservice IV*. Plans are in the works to run a line between the wrecks, and nitrox divers should be able to visit both in one dive.

Wreck Diving

Wreck diving can be safe and fascinating. Penetration of shipwrecks, however, is a skilled specialty and should not be attempted without proper training. Wrecks are often unstable; they can be silty, deep and disorienting. Use an experienced guide to view wrecks and the amazing coral communities that have developed on them.

7 Blackbeard's Eye & The Fence

A small volcanic island within sight of the airport, Saba offers an intriguing dive. On its rocky southeast side a large triangular sea cave leads back to a narrow, pebble-strewn tunnel in 10ft of water. Divers fin toward a murky green light (the eye) and surface in a small sunlit pool within the island. Conditions must be flat calm in order to dive here, as strong surge can make the passage rough. Unwary divers have been tossed onto the boulders that ring the inner pool.

After leaving the cave, turn right and head toward The Fence, a reef spur that juts out due south from the island. The spur rises from 30ft near shore to nearly break the surface. As you swim seaward, it gradually drops below 80ft, though most marine life flourishes above 60ft.

The reef slope is covered in large-cupped great star and brain corals and a variety of sponges, including rope, black ball, azure vase and giant barrel. Watch

Location: Saba Island

Depth Range: Surface-60ft+ (18m+)

Access: Boat

Expertise Rating: Intermediate

what you touch, as fire coral covers much of the substrate. Fish life includes lots of Spanish hogfish, queen and big French angels, mixed chromis, tangs, cottonwicks and pairs of butterflyfish. Dark-snouted hogfish and mutton snappers round out the larger species.

Head northwest across the sand to return toward the cave and the boat. You'll pass scattered star coral mounds. Cleaner gobies wait for customers atop the corals. Check beneath the mounds for bright orange elephant ear sponges and wary juvenile fish. Stingrays often rest on the sand.

Wait for flat calm seas to enter the tunnel's narrow eye.

8 Grain Wreck (*Grainton*)

Few wrecks in these waters approach the scale of the *Grainton*. Built by Chapman & Willan and launched in 1929, the 6,341-ton oceangoing freighter carried cargo across the Atlantic. She sank sometime prior to WWII, though the details of her demise have been lost over time. One account places the freighter at anchor, her holds packed with grain, when she began taking on water. The grain swelled, popping the deck seams, and the ship sank. It may not be true, but it makes a good predive story. After the war, Navy UDT teams used the wreck for deep-diving practice.

The site lies in open water about 30 minutes from shore, so currents are a very real concern. Wait for flat calm to dive here. Boats anchor at 105ft in the sand surrounding the wreck, and divers pull their way down the descent line. As the ship spans some 450ft from east to west, you'll only have time to visit either the bow or stern.

Time has been hard on the ship. Her sides are split and lie ribs up on the sand, and the superstructure long ago collapsed into the holds. Listing to port, only the bow and stern remain relatively intact. You'll likely start your tour amidships, where the engine block towers over the debris like a Roman arch, its three cylinder rods each as thick as a man's waist. Mixed chromis and cleaner wrasses mill atop the structure, which is coated in encrusting cup corals, sponges and hydroids. Just forward is the ship's massive boiler.

Location: South of Saba Island

Depth Range: 70-105ft (21-32m)

Access: Boat

Expertise Rating: Intermediate

Explore the open holds and as many crawl spaces as time allows, reserving plenty of air for a safety stop. The first divers down may catch sight of skittish reef sharks or passing turtles. Cottonwicks, creole wrasses, Spanish hogfish, Atlantic spadefish and large snappers roam throughout the wreck. Hiding within are groupers and hinds, bigeyes and longspine squirrelfish. Barracuda hover at the perimeter, waiting for lunch to swim by.

Hawksbill turtles sometimes shelter within the wreck.

9 | *Witconcrete II*

This U.S. Maritime Commission concrete barge was one of 22 built during WWII. Built in National City, California, and launched in 1943, she served as a fueling station for American warships in the South Pacific. After use in the Louisiana oil fields, she was brought down to join the West Indies Transport Co. fleet. Originally 375ft long, the ship lost 25ft of her stern to Hurricane Hugo in 1989 and was further damaged by Hurricane Marilyn in 1995. She was towed to her current spot and sunk on Oct. 3, 1996. The bow points to the northeast, the stern to the southwest.

Location: Southeast of Saba Island

Depth Range: 45-100ft (14-30m)

Access: Boat

Expertise Rating: Intermediate

Watch for pulsing moon jellyfish as you follow the anchor line to the main deck at about 60ft. Fifty-six feet wide and longer than a football field, the flattop deck extends out of sight no matter where you touch down. Algae coats the topside, supporting clouds of parrotfish, creole wrasses, tomtates and blue tangs. Bar jacks and mixed snappers school in the mid-water, while cleaner wrasses stay close to the deck. Watch for fire coral and hydroids along the ship's rails.

Amidships is a raised deckhouse where you might spot pairs of grazing French angelfish. Open hatches allow a peek into the 38ft deep fuel tanks, reinforced with 16ft thick concrete beams. Forward, two ladders lead up to the raised bow and anchor windlass. Drop down over the rail to admire her hull, coated in a variety of sponges and bright cup corals. Wooden fenders run the length of the hull, designed to protect the barge as ships pulled alongside to refuel.

Topping out at 45ft, debris on the raised stern deck shelters shifting schools of snappers. At the storm-damaged stern, four stories of inky black holds lie open to the sea, intertwined with old rope lines that sway in the current. Swim to the bottom to find schooling tomtates and yellowtail snappers. Hawksbill turtles often choose this spot to rest.

Sail Rock

According to popular island lore, this 125ft triangular rock 10 miles (16km) southwest of St. Thomas Harbor was mistaken for a hostile warship by a Revolution-era French schooner, which fired on the rock through the night. Below the surface a trio of submerged seamounts offer advanced divers rocketing drift dives amid schooling pelagics, sharks and colorful sponge growth. Winter swells may preclude diving here. The maximum depth is 90ft (27m).

10 Sprat Point

This spur-and-groove reef lies just outside St. Thomas Harbor. Its abundant marine life and proximity to the cruise ship docks make it a favorite among south side dive operators. Tradeoffs include strong surge and low visibility when tides pull silt out of the harbor. Don't fret if the vis is chunky, however, as most life here is on a macro level.

Location: East tip of Water Island

Depth Range: 25-50ft (8-15m)

Access: Boat

Expertise Rating: Novice

The reef stretches east-west, its sand grooves running perpendicular to shore. Boats moor at the base of the slope in 50ft of water, and divers head north to wander the aisles in search of marine life. The back reef levels off at about 25ft. You'll have time to explore about a half dozen or so channels before retracing your fin strokes to the boat.

Lining the channels are large heads of mountainous star coral, which form a series of overhangs, arches and swim-throughs decorated with orange ball and elephant ear sponges. As you explore, you may surprise large cubera snappers, Nassau groupers, orangespotted filefish, horned honeycomb cowfish or frilly spotted drums. Hawksbill turtles are also frequent visitors.

There's even more to see atop the coral spurs, as bluehead wrasses, parrotfish, mixed damsels, blue tangs, cleaner gobies, mixed chromis, silversides and juveniles of several species all vie for space. Sponges include black ball, tube and azure vase. You'll also find branches of elkhorn coral, as well as scattered pillar, large-cupped great star and fuzzy finger corals.

Down the shore a half mile southwest is the aptly named **Supermarket** (or **Limestone Reef**), another healthy spur-and-groove formation. The coral spurs here aren't as high profile, but marine life is every bit as varied.

A variety of colorful sponges line the ridges at this popular spur-and-groove reef.

11 Kennedy Wreck

In the mid-1980s this 200ft-plus barge served as a staging platform for launches to and from the visiting aircraft carrier USS *John F. Kennedy*. While being filled with water to bring her level to the carrier's hatches, she accidentally sank. Fitted with a concrete deck, the top-heavy barge flipped over as it went down, landing upside down on the sand at 65ft. The keel tops out at 50ft.

Location: Just outside St. Thomas Harbor

Depth Range: 50-65ft (15-20m)

Access: Boat

Expertise Rating: Novice

Opt for a night dive, when dozens of smooth trunkfish and stingrays congregate atop the wreck.

The east end of the wreck has collapsed into a tangled heap of hull plates and support beams that shelter hinds and graysbies, squirrelfish, cardinalfish and bigeyes. It's possible to swim through much of the wreck, with easy access to the outer hull. The west end is intact, and beyond it lies a large slab of the deck. Check the crawl space beneath the deck for more shade-loving species.

The hull sports a field of healthy gorgonians, mixed with rope and encrusting sponges and corals. Parrotfish graze on abundant algae alongside blue tangs, sergeant majors and banded and foureye butterflyfish. You'll find garden eels and yellowhead jawfish on the surrounding sand flats, while barracuda and yellowtail snappers sweep the water above the wreck.

Night diving on the barge is a real treat. Ranging in size from dinner plates to wading pools, several dozen stingrays gather atop the wreck. Smooth trunkfish also gather here in large numbers, pursing their pink lips at divers. Shine your dive light into the shadows to spot the golden pinpoints of red night shrimp eyes, and check the holds to find big cubera snappers and resting hawksbill turtles.

12 Navy Barges

These neighboring twin barges are among five sunk in the area following WWII. The vessels had been docked off the U.S. Navy submarine base in St. Thomas Harbor and used as enlisted men's quarters. Having outlived their usefulness, they were scuttled just outside the harbor. The shallow wrecks posed a hazard to shipping, however, so Navy UDT teams (precursors of the SEAL teams) were called in to use them for demolition practice. Dive teams from the base boated out to the barges, planted and set off charges of C-3, a plastic high explosive. The mangled hulls now support an array of marine life.

Dive boats tie up to moorings atop either barge. Divers typically tour the far wreck first, finishing at the barge beneath their boat for an easy ascent. Each covers an area roughly the size of

Location: Just off Limetree Beach

Depth Range: 25-40ft (8-12m)

Access: Boat

Expertise Rating: Novice

a basketball half court, with open beams and easy swim-throughs. The site is a macrophotographer's paradise.

Each hull is encrusted with colorful sponges and corals. Head topside on the wrecks to find juvenile wrasses and brown chromis, trumpetfish, parrotfish, big angelfish and lots of feather duster and Christmas tree worms. Closely inspect coral holes to find tiny blennies, with ugly mugs only a mother could love. Schoolmasters and grunts fill the holds.

Macro life seeks refuge within the shattered barges' many crawl spaces.

Check crawl spaces for squirrelfish, bigeyes, channel clinging crabs and spotted drums, and scan the surrounding sand for yellowhead jawfish and passing turtles and rays. Also look beneath the wreck for arrow crabs, banded coral shrimp and large lobsters. Watch where you stick your hand, though, as sea urchins are common.

The barges are also a good night dive, with lots of nocturnal species, including prowling octopuses. Beware of fire coral as you weave through the framework.

13 Armando's Paradise

Named for Armando Jenik, a veteran local diver and underwater cinematographer, this site features a wide, squat seamount that shelters an astounding variety of reef fish. Rising from 50ft at the mooring to within 10ft of the surface, the rock is bisected by a large channel and crisscrossed by several smaller cuts that offer tight but interesting swim-throughs. There are several winding passages on the far side of the rock and undercut ledges to the northeast, but you could happily spend all your time beneath the boat.

Fire coral and sea urchins are common in the shallows, so be careful as you descend. The rocky substrate is painted in encrusting corals and sponges, capped with gorgonians and carpeted in algae. You'll definitely spot cleaner

Location: SW of Bolongo Bay

Depth Range: 10-50ft (3-15m)

Access: Boat

Expertise Rating: Novice

wrasses, mixed chromis and damsels, harlequin bass, fairy basslets, sergeant majors, blue tangs and bright parrotfish. Lucky divers may spot soapfish, orangspotted filefish or thumb-sized redlip blennies. The site is a nursery of sorts for fry and juvenile fish.

Corals and sponges are larger on the surrounding reef, featuring plate and star corals and giant barrel sponges. Boasting big orange elephant ear sponges, the outlying ledges shelter nurse sharks, lobsters and channel clinging crabs.

14 *Cartanza Señora* & Buck Island Cove

Not to be confused with the national monument off St. Croix, this Buck Island is a small, rocky national wildlife refuge with a lighthouse and three beaches. An easy 15- to 20-minute boat ride south of St. Thomas, it's a favorite destination among south side dive shops. Perfect for students and novices, its west cove offers year-round sheltered diving.

The centerpiece is the *Cartanza Señora*, a 190ft interisland freighter towed here

Location: West end of Buck Island

Depth Range: 20-60ft (6-18m)

Access: Boat

Expertise Rating: Novice

and sunk as an artificial reef in 1979. A series of hurricanes have since broken the wreck into three pieces, but it remains a marine life magnet. You'll first reach the midsection, split open and littered with stacked bags of cement. The bow and stern are within sight to the south and west, respectively.

Darting between the coral- and sponge-encrusted sections are blue chromis, creole wrasses, brown damsels, snappers and grunts. You may also find nervous sergeant majors, desperately guarding their purple egg masses smeared on the hull. Visit the cleaning stations alongside the wreck, and check crawl spaces for copper sweepers and invertebrates such as arrow crabs and brittle stars. The surrounding sand flats are home to colonies of yellowhead jawfish and juveniles of many species.

On the south side of the cove is **Wye Reef**, a jumble of boulders that bottoms out on the sand at 60ft. Look hard to find remains of the steamship *Wye*, a sister ship to the infamous RMS *Rhone*. To the north are **Tejo's Reef**, a favorite with snorkelers, and **Buck Island Point**, a classic spur-and-groove reef with its own mooring just around the corner.

Save the Wreck

The *Cartanza Señora* has a hazy past. Even its name is in question—some still refer to it as the *Cartanser Senior*. Rumors surfaced about the legality of its last cargo after the ship was abandoned by captain and crew in the late 1970s. Eventually, the batteries ran down, the bilge pumps failed and she took on water and sank in West Gregerie Channel, a main shipping lane into St. Thomas Harbor. The Corps of Engineers made plans to demolish this "navigational hazard."

Before that could happen, on March 30, 1979, the Italian cruise liner *Angelina Lauro* caught fire and sank in St. Thomas Harbor, and a massive floating crane was shipped to the territory to refloat her. Seeing an opportunity, local divers held an underwater "Save the Wreck" fund-raiser and paid the crane operators several thousand dollars to also raise the *Cartanza*. The ship was towed to Buck Island that spring and sunk as an artificial reef.

15 André's Reef & Dive Flag Rock

These neighboring sites share the same wide reef slope on Buck's north side. The west end is named for veteran local diver and submarine captain André Webber. On the east end a flat shoreline rock sports a diagonal crack that does suggest a dive flag (have your boat crew point it out). Moorings are on the back reef in about 25ft. Swim north from either mooring to reach the reef crest at 35ft.

The moderately steep slope is covered in lobed star corals, scattered staghorn and pillar corals and a wide variety of sponges. Swirling atop the corals are clouds of mixed chromis, damsels and cleaner wrasses. Keep an eye out for

Location: North side of Buck Island

Depth Range: 25-75ft (8-23m)

Access: Boat

Expertise Rating: Novice

smooth trunkfish, foureye butterflyfish, feathery golden crinoids and purple-spotted Pederson cleaner shrimp, which gyrate wildly to attract customers. Parrotfish nibble on the abundant algae, while yellowtail snappers and silvery jacks cruise overhead. Check the reef crevices to find rock hinds, spotted drums and several moray species. Alert divers may spot an octopus or perhaps a passing reef shark.

The sand bottom slopes gently westward from 65ft off Dive Flag Rock to about 75ft off André's. Scattered along the sand just off the reef are the remains of a cement mixer, minus the truck. The scattered machine parts sport a range of sponges and encrusting organisms and offer shelter to juvenile reef species and the occasional resting hawksbill turtle.

As you descend the reef slope, watch for moray eels.

16 Submarine Alley (Snapper Valley)

Within sight of the Buck Island light, this site is the cruising ground of the Atlantis sightseeing submarine, which dives here up to nine times a day, sometimes surprising groups of visiting divers. The mooring is in 40ft of water. You'll swim north down the reef slope to reach a series of broad coral mounds that climb

Location: East side of Buck Island

Depth Range: 40-80ft (12-24m)

Access: Boat

Expertise Rating: Intermediate

from 80ft to about 50ft. "Four-lane" sand alleys crisscross the mounds. More than 10 mounds stretch out over the sand, but time will limit your tour to two or three of them.

Large yellowtail snappers greet you at the mooring and follow you throughout your dive, hence the alternate name. You'll reach the first sand alley at 70ft and follow it east to a sandy intersection at 80ft, marked by the remains of a sail-boat that sank during a hurricane. From here you'll wander down several more alleys and cross the mounds. Large heads of mountainous and lobed star corals anchor the gentle slopes, mixed with plate, finger and spherical starlet and brain corals. Gorgonians sway in the shallows, and you'll find a range of sponges throughout the site.

The mounds attract mixed chromis and damsels, cleaner wrasses, Spanish

The 65ft sightseeing submarine can be a startling sight for the unwary diver.

hogfish, parrotfish and blue tangs. Check reef nooks for squirrelfish, lobsters and moray eels, especially around the lobed star corals. Stingrays and spotted goatfish root in the sand, and several large barracuda cruise the alleys. Also keep watch for a 65ft, 320,000-pound white submarine.

17   Joe's Jam (Coral Bowl)

Inshore of Submarine Alley is this wide bowl of raised mountainous and lobed star corals trimmed with plate and cactus corals, fuzzy finger and pillar corals, the odd staghorn cluster, branching tube sponges, big sea fans and giant sea rods. The star corals are deeply undercut in places and shelter bright orange elephant ear sponges. Three moorings mark the west lip of the bowl, which starts at 30ft and slopes to sand below 70ft.

Fish life is equally healthy, with typical crowds of parrotfish, grunts and tangs, mixed chromis and damsels, creole wrasses, butterflyfish and hamlets. Check the undercuts for schoolmasters, squirrelfish, graysbies and hinds, copper sweepers, fairy basslets, rock beauties and lurking barracuda. They also harbor resting nurse sharks and turtles. Yellowtail

Location: North side of Capella Island

Depth Range: 30-70ft+ (9-21m+)

Access: Boat

Expertise Rating: Novice

snappers and bar jacks cruise the perimeter, and you may spot lobsters and feathery golden crinoids in the reef nooks.

You can stay relatively shallow here and find lots of surprises. Keep an eye out for pairs of orangespotted and whitespotted filefish, harlequin bass, cute little balloonfish and passing rays. Search the lobed star corals for such beautiful eels as the goldentail and chain morays. Also check out the cleaning stations, run by Pederson and banded coral shrimp, juvenile wrasses and neon gobies.

Healthy star coral mounds ring this site, providing hiding places for puffers and other species.

18 Frenchman's Cap (Frenchcap Cay)

Weather conditions, strong currents and its distance from shore often thwart plans to dive on this rocky cay a 30-minute boat ride south of St. Thomas. Some shops rule it out altogether. Check with dive operators on St. Thomas' East End and on St. John. If you are able to go, the cay offers a few options.

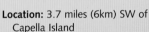

Location: 3.7 miles (6km) SW of Capella Island

Depth Range: 35-95ft (11-29m)

Access: Boat

Expertise Rating: Intermediate

Frenchman's Cap offers divers an array of canyons, ledges, caves and pinnacles.

On the north side is a vertical cut in the rock that opens into a shallow sun-lit chamber known as **The Cathedral**, its walls coated in shade-loving cup corals and sponges. The sandy floor bottoms out at about 35ft.

Along the northeast side are the **Ledges**, a 300ft long series of deeply undercut ledges, with several fun swim-throughs. Divers often spot lobsters and resting nurse sharks under the ledges, while turtles and eagle rays sometimes cruise by in the blue water. Maximum depth is about 65ft.

Off the southeast tip of the cay is the **Pinnacle**, actually a tight grouping of sponge- and coral-coated spires that rise from the seafloor at 95ft and top out at about 45ft. Advanced divers may have to battle the current, though visibility sometimes approaches 200ft. Clouds of fish swirl atop the formation, attracting hungry jacks and barracuda. This is another good spot to see eagle rays.

19 Cow & Calf

Protected within the St. James Marine Reserve, these neighboring rocks just break the surface. Their names are reflective of the region's whaling past. The larger of the two (Cow) is less than a quarter mile west of its smaller "off-spring" (Calf). Underwater, the sites are riddled with tunnels, arches, canyons and undercut ledges, as well as reeftops capped with swaying gorgonians and a variety of sponges. Beware the fire coral at both sites. Moorings lie southwest and northwest of Cow and due north of Calf.

Location: Just west of Great St. James

Depth Range: Surface-45ft (14m)

Access: Boat

Expertise Rating: Novice

Cow is the best known of the two. Divers often compare the site to a play-ground or miniature golf course, and navigating its many twists and turns is like a children's game. You'll play follow the leader, enter-ing single file through a short tunnel that opens on a perfect stone arch. Over your left shoulder is a small cave, while to the right is a longer tunnel that leads to the famed "Champagne Cork." One by one, divers approach the end of the tunnel, wait for the surge, then pop toward the surface in a shower of bubbles.

Drop back down and swim through a slot canyon,

Cow rock is a playful maze of colorful swim-throughs.

then circle back clockwise to the beginning. As the site maxes out at 40ft, you'll have plenty of time to explore. Damselfish, tangs, wrasses, angelfish and butterflyfish, jawfish and lots of juveniles swim out in the open, while the innermost nooks shelter squirrelfish, grunts and snappers, scorpionfish, lobsters and large groupers.

Calf offers a series of dramatic ledges, wide canyons and large caves. The deeply undercut ledges are coated in encrusting organisms, including colorful sponges and delicate cups of golden tubastrea. Fish life is similar to that on Cow, but on a grander scale, with vast schools, more big fish and legions of lobsters.

20 Ledges of Little St. James

Little St. James was recently sold to a real-estate developer with rumored plans to build on the island. The fish already have a condo of sorts off the southwest point, where tiers of deeply undercut ledges shelter a colorful mix of marine life. This is a great site for novices, as it's fairly shallow and protected from the prevailing currents. It's also fun to explore.

Location: SW point of island

Depth Range: 20-30ft (6-9m)

Access: Boat

Expertise Rating: Novice

Three moorings lie in 25ft of water beneath a boulder field just north of the point. Plentiful algae attracts lots of fish, from parrotfish and goatfish to yellow-

tail snappers, rock hinds, damsels and schools of grazing blue tangs. Drop to the bottom for a look, taking care to avoid numerous stands of mustard-tinged fire coral. Also common are isolated pillar

Mixed grunts and yellow goatfish part ways for a passing diver.

corals. Unlike other hard corals, this tall species looks fuzzy, as its polyps feed by day, not night.

The ledges are a short swim south along the base of the reef. You'll reach one ledge at around 20ft, followed by a mini swim-through canyon, then multiple tiers between 20 and 35ft. Too tight to accommodate a diver, the ledges are undercut some 15 to 20ft. They're coated with encrusting corals and sponges and topped with lush gorgonians. Sergeant majors and blue chromis crowd the reeftop, while the ledges are a hang-out for lobsters and other reef species, including flirtatious rock beauties.

21 Coki Beach

Don't let the crowded beach scene throw you. Less than 100 yards from shore is a perfect fringing reef for divers of all experience levels. Snorkelers can drift amid hundreds of hand-fed sergeant majors, while nondivers can visit adjacent Coral World marine park. Everyone is happy. The best entry point is opposite Coki Beach Dive Club, operating out of an old U.S. mail truck beside the road.

There are actually two reefs here—one stretching east, the other west, a sand flat between them populated by garden eels. Make your choice based on the current. In calm conditions head toward Coral World and the east reef. A maximum depth of 50ft means plenty of time to explore.

Location: East End, near Coral World

Depth Range: 15-50ft (5-15m)

Access: Shore

Expertise Rating: Novice

The slope is carpeted in gorgonians that tower over star and brain coral mounds and a variety of sponges. Fish life features yellowtail snappers, bar jacks, yellow goatfish, chromis, tangs, grunts and parrotfish. Thousands of tiny masked gobies hover atop the corals, while rock hinds hide beneath them. Trumpetfish lurk amid the sea rods. Check inside sponges for arrow crabs, brittle stars, cleaner gobies and Pederson cleaner shrimp. Arrange in advance for night dives, which star a new cast of characters, including tiny balloonfish and prowling octopuses.

Draped down the east slope, the aquarium's water intake pipes mark the turn-around point. A short swim out on the sand are "Pete's Pipes," a collection of old intake pipes, mesh cages and boat parts that shelter tomtates and juvenile yellowtail snappers. Keep an eye out for passing stingrays and turtles. The shallow return to the beach doubles as your safety stop.

Just off the beach is a thriving coral reef.

Pillsbury Sound & St. John Dive Sites

St. John is where St. Thomians go to "get away from it all." One look from the air is enough to understand why. Three-fifths of the island is protected within Virgin Islands National Park. Development within the park is limited to park service facilities, existing private homes and a few scattered plantation ruins. The slopes are otherwise free from human intervention, with rolling green hills, broad sandy beaches and healthy fringing reefs. Hiking trails crisscross this landscape, taking in a variety of terrain. Outdoor enthusiasts can also ride horses and donkeys or rent sea kayaks.

On the West End, Cruz Bay is the center of activity, with a decent range of boutiques, restaurants and watersports centers. Nightlife centers on a handful of laid-back bars. It's a 20-minute ride via passenger or car ferry to Red Hook, 4 miles (6km) west across Pillsbury Sound. On the East End, Coral Bay is the other main population center, with limited dining options and only one dive operator, St. John Dive Adventures.

Driving the island is an easy prospect, as there are only two main arteries between Cruz and Coral Bays. North Shore Road (Route 20) will take you to the famed string of St. John beaches. Avoid the crowds at Trunk Bay and instead head to Cinnamon Bay or Leinster Bay, the latter one of the territory's best snorkeling spots. Centerline Road (Route 10) climbs up over the mountains and back down into Coral Bay. Remembering to stay left is not the greatest road hazard here—that distinction is left to the legions of donkeys and mixed livestock wandering the roads, not to mention the occasional iguana or mongoose.

Coral Bay anchors St. John's East End, beyond which lie the British Virgin Islands.

Pillsbury Sound & St. John Dive Sites

	Good Snorkeling	Novice	Intermediate	Advanced
22 Arches & Tunnels of Thatch			●	
23 *Maj. Gen. Rogers*			●	
24 Grass Cay		●		
25 Mounds at Mingo	●	●		
26 Lovango Cay		●		
27 Congo Cay	●		●	
28 Carval Rock				●
29 Lind Point		●		
30 Witch's Hat		●		
31 Cocoloba		●		
32 Maple Leaf			●	
33 Booby Rock		●		
34 Eagle Shoal			●	
35 Flanagan Reef	●		●	

Mongooses ... in the Caribbean?

The mongoose is a popular icon of island life, lending its name and image to such landmarks as Mongoose Junction mall in Cruz Bay. That wasn't always the case.

Brought here centuries ago by Danish plantation owners to control sugarcane-eating rats, the mongoose was alas a heavy sleeper, while the rats were nocturnal. The fleet-footed forager feasted instead on fruit, chickens, eggs and other necessary staples, drawing the ire of island farmers. Today NPS officials keep mongoose numbers in check to protect the eggs and hatchlings of threatened bird, turtle, reptile and amphibian species.

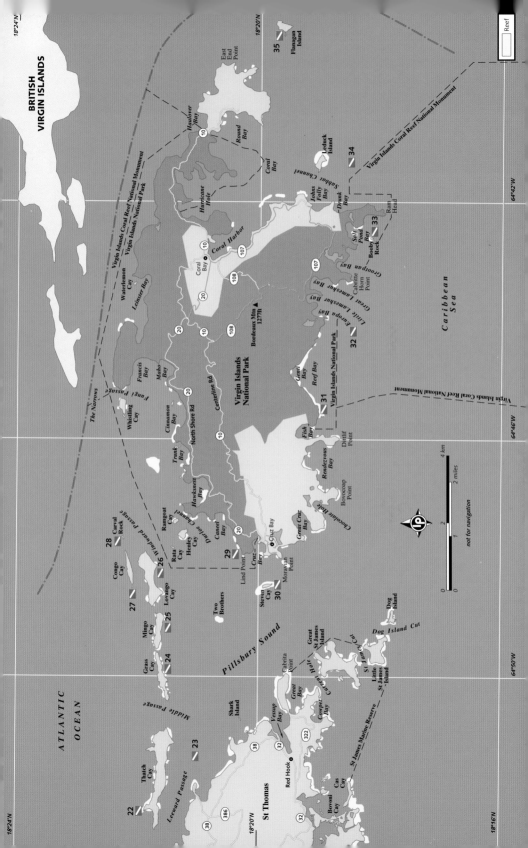

22 Arches & Tunnels of Thatch

In a cove bordered by steep craggy cliffs, this site is renowned for a series of black rock arches and lava tubes that attest to the region's volcanic past. Bring a dive light to navigate and to appreciate the colorful growth that coats the tunnel walls. Winter swells bring strong surge, making passage through the longer tubes hazardous. Watch for fire coral through-out the site.

Location: NW end of Thatch Cay

Depth Range: 25-40ft (8-12m)

Access: Boat

Expertise Rating: Intermediate

The mooring is in 25ft just west of a rocky spur that breaks the surface. Divers head northeast toward the point across a field of swaying gorgonians. You'll enter the formations through a wide arch encrusted in sponges and bright cup corals. Swimming single file, divers turn right and head up a pebble-strewn groove to the first tunnel entrance. Running some 60ft through the rock, with a dogleg left about halfway through, this is the longest tunnel and the one most susceptible to surge. If the passage looks rough, your divemaster will bypass it altogether.

The tunnel exits at 30ft on a wide sand flat. Wend your way counterclockwise past big boulders and gorgonian patches to the next tunnel, a rectangular hallway about 30ft long. Cup corals and sponges also coat its crooked walls. You'll emerge in another rocky groove, then turn left through a notch in the wall. Avoid the fire coral as you swim through a small round arch and narrow slot into an adjacent channel. Head left to find the final short tunnel, which exits in the groove leading back to the first wide arch.

Butterflyfish, damsels, parrotfish and tangs hunker down amid the gorgonians, while vast clouds of silversides sweep the reef, stalked by long, sleek tarpon. Check the star coral mounds for cleaner gobies, and inspect the many reef crevices to find moray eels and spiny lobsters.

You'll swim single file through black rock lava tubes.

23 | *Maj. Gen. Rogers*

Easy access, shallow depths, lots of fish and 30-plus years of marine growth make the *Maj. Gen. Rogers* a popular site with both operators and divers. As the ship lies in mid-channel between St. Thomas and Thatch Cay, it regularly experiences strong currents. Boats tie to a mooring atop either the bow or stern, and divers descend the line to the deck at 45ft.

Built in 1940 by Spedden Shipbuilding in Baltimore, the 135ft Army freighter was named after Maj. Gen. Harry Lovejoy Rogers, the 25th quartermaster general of the U.S. Following service in WWII, the ship hauled cargo for a series of owners. In 1972 its final owner obtained permission to sink the aging ship as an artificial reef. Tragically, one of the men hired to scuttle the ship died when it sank prematurely, pulling him under. The site is a living memorial to his efforts.

Location: Leeward Passage, south of Thatch Cay

Depth Range: 40-65ft (12-20m)

Access: Boat

Expertise Rating: Intermediate

Pointing due east, the ship sits upright on the sand in 65ft of water. The hull is encrusted in colorful sponges and orange cup corals, which open in the current like a field of dandelions. Keep watch for fairy basslets, juvenile angelfish and tiny blennies, as well as clusters of fluorescent blue bell tunicates. The propeller is particularly photogenic, boasting a thick beard of encrusting corals and sponges.

Though the superstructure is gone, the deck plating and machinery remain.

Within easy reach of dive operators on both islands, the *Maj. Gen. Rogers* is a favorite site.

You'll find the steering mechanism in the aft hold, the engine amidships and a spare prop in the forward hold. Coral growth on deck is limited to brain corals toward the bow and fire coral along the rails. Hands off is a good policy, as hydroids and bristle worms are also present. Barracuda stalk thick clouds of silversides atop the wreck, while mixed chromis, cleaner wrasses, tomtates, sergeant majors and other damsels mill about the deck. Check the holds for long stovepipe sponges, snappers and grunts, lobsters and large crabs.

About 200ft off the bow is the wreck of the *Mary King*, a 110ft self-propelled barge. Nitrox divers should have no problem taking in both ships on one tank.

24 Grass Cay

Location: Between Thatch & Mingo Cays

Depth Range: 15-65ft (5-20m)

Access: Boat

Expertise Rating: Novice

Marine life flourishes along the cay's lee shore.

The fringing reef south of Grass Cay boasts some of the healthiest corals in the territory. It slopes in stages from about 15ft to the sand between 60 and 65ft. Scattered atop the sand are several large star coral mounds thick with gorgonians, sponges, invertebrates and colorful reef fish. Depending on your entry point and dive operator, you'll hear several names used in conjunction with the mounds, including **Mary's Mounds** and **Grassco Junction**. This is a good spot to watch corals spawn in summer. Tucked into the shallows is **The Classroom**, a sandy training site.

A trio of moorings runs east-west, parallel to shore. The westernmost buoy marks **The Gardens**, or **Al's Cut**, which takes in the reef slope, a high-profile spur and several of the coral mounds. From the mooring, groups typically follow the spur south, then swim east from its tip to the coral mounds. The return trip takes you up and over the spur. This raised reef features lobed and mountainous star corals atop sand. Gorgonians sway amid the mounds, which include smaller heads of great star, starlet, finger, pillar and staghorn corals. Rope, tube, black ball and azure vase sponges fill in the gaps the deeper you go. Look for orange elephant ear sponges beneath the mounds.

Parrotfish, goatfish, creole wrasses, tangs, mixed chromis and damsels busily search for food, while hamlets, grunts,

snappers, squirrelfish, lobsters and feathery golden crinoids shelter beneath the reef. Peek beneath the mounds to find lurking barracuda or resting nurse sharks and turtles. Morays often hide in the lobed star mounds. The deeper reaches support barrel sponges and deepwater sea fans, which look somewhat like trees in winter. Keep watch for rays and passing pelagics out on the sand.

Sex & the Single Polyp

While many aspects of coral reproduction baffle scientists, the timing of a coral spawning event is precise. Seven to 10 nights after the first full moon in August, the Virgin reefs explode in an upside-down snowstorm of coral sperm and eggs. Upon release, the procreative packets float to the surface, where they separate and mingle. Sometimes the release is slow and steady, other times the surface is thick with slick. The fertilized eggs hatch into larvae, which lead a planktonic existence before settling down on the reef to resume the cycle.

25 Mounds at Mingo

This site offers both a healthy reef slope and the namesake mounds on a sandy bottom. A highlight is the wide variety of sponges. Three moorings run east-west along the back reef in 15ft of water. Divers typically swim south down the slope and meander amid the coral heads before heading slowly back up to the boat. Snorkelers will appreciate the sheltered location, as currents are absent and visibility is usually excellent.

The moderate reef slope is practically paved with lobed star corals. Juvenile

Location: South side of Mingo Cay

Depth Range: 15-50ft (5-15m)

Access: Boat

Expertise Rating: Novice

fish of many species populate the reeftop, along with busy blue chromis, bluehead wrasses, sergeant majors and other damselfish, grunts, hamlets and nibbling parrotfish. Look closely to find leopard-spotted flamingo tongues, which graze on sea fans atop the reef. Also tricky to spot are morays, which hide in the coral heads. The deeper you go, the more sponges you'll find, starting with rope and tube sponges, then solitary vases and giant barrels.

The slope ends abruptly on sand flats at 50ft. Scattered a couple hundred feet out on the sand, the low-profile mounds vary from car-sized to house-sized. Each is saturated with colorful sponge life, gorgonians, deepwater sea fans, small coral heads and encrusting corals. Fish life includes fairy basslets, more damselfish and parrotfish, roaming schools of blue tangs and an occasional striking angelfish. Rays and pelagics cruise the blue water. Wide-angle photographers will have no shortage of subject matter.

26 Lovango Cay

Rumor has it this scrub-covered cay was named for a bordello once based on the island, hence "love an' go." As the dive site lies toward the end of the cay, visibility may suffer and currents can be a factor, especially in winter months. The site is often done as a drift dive. A lone mooring sits in 15ft of water, and the reef slopes gradually southwest to a sand bottom at about 40ft.

Sand paths crisscross between lobed star corals and the odd staghorn amid fields of swaying sea rods and plumes. The star corals shelter several residents, including lobsters, moray eels and rough fileclams, which extend delicate white tentacles to feed on microscopic prey.

Location: South side of cay

Depth Range: 15-40ft (5-12m)

Access: Boat

Expertise Rating: Novice

Sponges are plentiful, including rope, tube, vase and barrel species.

Turtles, rays and big African pompano sometimes cruise by, while parrotfish, tangs, damsels and hamlets focus on their food—you'll hear crunching as the parrotfish scrape algae from the coral. Divers with keen eyes will find trumpetfish and tiny slender filefish hiding amid purple porous sea rods, as well as spindly arrow crabs, which dance together at the base of giant sea rods. You may also spot smooth trunkfish and pairs of foureye butterflyfish.

Careful observers may notice telltale humps along the sandy bottom, giving away the presence of bowl-sized red heart urchins. These short-spined urchins look somewhat like furry pincushions. You may also find their bleached white skeletons atop the sand.

Look closely to spot juvenile smooth trunkfish.

27 Congo Cay

The shallow sandy channel between Lovango and Congo Cays is a favorite stop among diving and snorkeling operators, while craggy cliffs on Congo's north side continue underwater in a dramatic drop-off. The current and surge will dictate your profile. Three moorings skirt the southwest end. Beneath them a field of gorgonians slopes to sand between 35 and 50ft. Follow this reef line west to the ridge of uplifted pinnacles that mark the point. On rough days this may be as far as you get.

Rounding the point, you'll soon reach a pinnacle that rises from 40ft to break the surface. As you head deeper, check reef nooks for lobsters, moray eels and nurse sharks. You'll pass a nearly closed swim-through near the surface, then more boulders before you reach two

Location: Just north of Lovango Cay

Depth Range: 25-85ft (8-26m)

Access: Boat

Expertise Rating: Intermediate

massive upended slabs that form a box canyon. The slabs magnify any surge, rocking you and thousands of silversides back and forth. Keep an eye out for hunting tarpon and jacks.

Beyond this point the reef drops sheer from the surface to 60ft, then slopes to the sand between 80 and 85ft. The base of the cliff is littered with large fallen slabs and boulders coated with gorgonians, mat zoanthids, low-profile corals,

Caribbean spiny lobsters are among the critters that populate Congo's steep north side.

barrel and orange ball sponges and deep-water sea fans. Watch the blue for turtles and graceful eagle rays.

Back beneath the boat, a mix of common reef fish dart amid the gorgonians, while flamingo tongue mollusks munch greedily on the sea fans. The sand flats support goatfish, lizardfish, tilefish, conchs and flounders. Sift the sand to uncover red heart urchins, sand dollars and striking elliptical sunrise tellin shells.

28 Carval Rock

Connected to Congo Cay by a submarine ridge, this is actually a series of adjacent rocks. Serving as a nesting site for terns and other seabirds, the main rock is a dramatic jumble of fractured stone and balancing boulders. The site is exposed to currents and northerly swells, making diving here an iffy prospect, especially in winter.

Location: Just east of Congo Cay

Depth Range: 20-80ft (6-24m)

Access: Boat

Expertise Rating: Advanced

A shallow fringing reef on the south side sports a carpet of gorgonians and sponges, which attract the usual reef suspects, including parrotfish, chromis, creole wrasses and sergeant majors. But the real highlight is the sheer north face, which plunges below 80ft—one of the few drop-offs outside of St. Croix. Narrow cuts and swim-throughs allow divers to meander back and forth, though rough seas often make that difficult. Vast shoals of silversides gather here, attracting large, hungry tarpon. Watch the blue for pelagics and rays.

When conditions allow, Carval Rock is a thrilling drift dive amid flashing shoals of silversides.

29 Lind Point

In national park waters just around the corner from busy Cruz Bay, this site sees lots of boat traffic, from passing ferries to the charter sailboats that regularly moor here. Be particularly careful when surfacing. Though storm swells have damaged the coral cover somewhat, prevailing currents attract abundant fish life.

Location: Just north of Cruz Bay

Depth Range: 20-60ft (6-18m)

Access: Boat

Expertise Rating: Novice

Divers enter on the sandy back reef in 20ft of water, then drift west along the slope, which bottoms out between 50ft and 60ft at the point. The currents support deepwater sea fans and a variety of sponges. Angelfish sample this sponge smorgasbord, while tangs, parrotfish and damsels forage for algae tidbits and tigertail sea cucumbers stretch from the reef to vacuum the sandy seafloor.

Night dives are a busy affair. Your dive light will draw frenetic swarms of fish fry. Sweep the reef with your light to spot smooth trunkfish, spiny and slipper lobsters, moray eels and translucent reef squid. Hermit crabs scurry along the bottom between discarded wine bottles. Near the point is the wreck of a small sailboat encrusted in sponges and deepwater sea fans. Check inside for big crabs, nurse sharks or the resident green moray.

At night Caribbean reef squid glow under the beam of your dive light.

30 Witch's Hat

Just outside Cruz Bay on the south tip of Steven Cay, a pointy-tipped rock marks Witch's Hat, where wheatlike fields of sea plumes and giant sea rods flank a shallow crescent of undercut ledges. The ledges stretch some 200ft and are topped with a mix of sponges, corals and gorgonians. Their undersides sport bright cup corals, elephant ear sponges and deepwater sea fans. Watch what you touch, as fire coral coats most surfaces.

Strong currents sweep the site, carrying nutrients that support a wide array of reef fish. You may log more species here than at all other sites combined. Darting about the reeftop are schools of blue tangs and creole wrasses, butterflyfish and parrotfish, cleaner wrasses, blue and brown chromis, solitary Spanish hogfish and trumpetfish, legions of

Location: South tip of Steven Cay

Depth Range: 15-30ft (5-9m)

Access: Boat

Expertise Rating: Novice

sergeant majors and other damsels. Beneath the ledges, fish competing for fin room include many juveniles, as well as big gray, queen and French angelfish, mixed snappers and grunts, goatfish, squirrelfish and bigeyes, porcupinefish, spotted drums and fairy basslets. Look carefully to spot hiding lobsters and pancake-flat peacock flounders. A maximum depth of 30ft means plenty of time to browse.

Fish flit atop the ledges, while the undersides are ablaze with encrusting sponges and cup corals.

31 | Cocoloba

This shallow sandy site within national park waters serves as an Open Water training area and makes a fun second dive. It takes its name from Cocoloba Cay, the rocky islet just west of the anchorage, which is covered with the namesake sea grape trees (*Coccoloba uvifera*). A spur-and-groove reef starts between the cay and shore and stretches east, breaking up

Location: South shore, west of Reef Bay

Depth Range: 5-30ft (2-9m)

Access: Boat

Expertise Rating: Novice

Cocoloba's sheltered overhangs are a good spot to find resting nurse sharks.

into a network of scattered reef mounds, swim-throughs and undercut ledges.

Navigation is deceptively difficult here, as the depth remains constant and the formations twist and turn like an English boxwood maze, with a number of narrow passages, arches and sandy cul-de-sacs. Mountainous star corals line the undercut spurs, which are wreathed in gorgonians. The shallows boast large brain and lobed star corals amid wide purple sea fans and patches of golden mat zoanthids.

You'll find all the common reef species, including tangs, parrotfish, chromis and butterflyfish. Look beneath the ledges for big queen and French angelfish and tiny fairy basslets, which swim with their bellies to the ceiling. Bigger fish include snappers and stout nurse sharks, which rest under the ledges. Check the sand for goatfish, motionless lizardfish and the beautiful sunrise tellin, an oval shell that sports a colorful sunburst pattern. Park regulations apply—do not remove or harm any marine life.

32   Maple Leaf

Just east of Reef Bay, this large offshore reef fans out seaward, dropping from about 45ft on the back reef to the sand at 80ft. Sand channels crisscross the formation like veins on a leaf. Garden eels populate the current-swept deep end. Divers are dropped from a "live boat," then picked up following their dive. The site lies within the new Virgin Islands Coral Reef National Monument.

Location: South shore, between Reef & Lameshur Bays

Depth Range: 45-80ft (14-24m)

Access: Boat

Expertise Rating: Novice

The moderate reef slope is blanketed with lush corals and gorgonians. No one species dominates here—spheres of starlet and brain coral grow alongside mountainous, lobed and great star, pillar and cactus, finger, pencil, flower and sheet corals. Larger mounds of mountainous star coral line the sand channels, forming delicate overhangs and swimthroughs that sport orange elephant ear and orange ball sponges. Look for such typical shade-loving species as lobsters, feathery golden crinoids, fairy basslets, squirrelfish, schoolmasters and other large snappers.

Amid the field of purple rope sponges and gorgonians atop the reef, you'll find the usual mixed chromis and damsels, parrotfish, tangs and tiny copper-spotted masked gobies. Also watch for passing jacks, yellowtail snappers and hordes of creole wrasses. Stealing the scene are cruising barracuda, pretty rock beauties and French angelfish, not to mention pairs of 60-pound permits sure to impress any diver.

From the depths at Maple Leaf, an orange ball sponge reflects light like a miniature sun.

33 Booby Rock

This small volcanic rock in national park waters is named for the brown booby, a bird that traditionally nested here. Tumbled stone slabs continue underwater, forming undercut ledges, caves, pinnacles and canyons. You'll have time to circumnavigate the rock. Southeast swells can make the boat trip rough, so dive operators wait for calm days to visit.

Location: South shore, west of Ram Head

Depth Range: 15-50ft (5-15m)

Access: Boat

Expertise Rating: Novice

The mooring is in 30ft of water on the northwest side. Moving counterclockwise, you'll start at a field of large boulders on sand along the west side. Gorgonians coat most surfaces, along with colorful rope sponges. Trumpetfish hover beside the sea rods, while Nassau groupers and Spanish hogfish hole up amid the boulders. Several rocks are capped with healthy stands of pillar coral. Be wary of fire coral in the shallows.

To the south, several sharp rocks stand on end, forming small pinnacles that break the surface. Just around the corner is a small cave filled with silversides and fairy basslets, black coral bushes and perhaps a channel clinging crab. Peer in from the outside to avoid damaging its fragile residents. The east side is largely undercut, a great place to hunt for lobsters and large nurse sharks. Check the reef nooks for hinds and giant anemones.

You'll return to the mooring through several wide channels that cut across the north side.

Typical reef species in the shallows give way to surprises in deeper water. Keep an eye out for colorful queen trig-

Pea-sized juvenile smooth trunkfish defy belief.

Tektite & Her Deepness

At the dawn of the space program, underwater habitats were used to research the psychological effects of extended isolation and the physiological effects of breathing compressed air. In a joint effort by NASA, the Department of the Interior and the Navy, *Tektite* was ballasted to the seafloor at 50ft (15m) in St. John's Greater Lameshur Bay. In early 1969 four "aquanauts" spent a two months conducting biological studies from the habitat while being monitored by behavioral scientists. In July 1970 a second team of aquanauts spent two weeks aboard *Tektite*. This team comprised five women, led by "Her Deepness" Sylvia Earle, who would later become chief scientist at NOAA.

gerfish, big queen and French angels, spotted drums, honeycomb cowfish and all ages of smooth trunkfish. Juveniles of the latter species are black with white polka dots and no bigger than a grape—a comical sight for the lucky diver.

34 Eagle Shoal

Seldom dived by visitors or locals, Eagle Shoal is considered the Holy Grail of East End diving. What makes diving here so difficult is its distance from Cruz Bay and its exposure to prevailing southeasterly swells. What makes it irresistible is topography highlighted by deep ledges and a magical cave that has hosted underwater weddings. Passing bull sharks add to the excitement.

Location: Between Ram Head & Leduck Island

Depth Range: 5-50ft (2-15m)

Access: Boat

Expertise Rating: Intermediate

Most divers head straight for the cave, known as "The Cathedral," on the northeast side of the shoal. Wide passages lead into the central hall at 40ft. Kneel amid boulders on the sandy floor while you admire a flat, low ceiling coated in a colorful fresco of encrusting sponges and orange cup corals. Shine your dive light on bright sponges that hang from a rocky chandelier at the center of the room. To one side is the sanctuary's "rose window," a circular skylight some

At the heart of Eagle Shoal is "The Cathedral," a skylit cave that has hosted several weddings.

20ft across—often filled with thousands of shimmering silversides. Visitors may include barracuda and groupers or passing jacks and permits.

Swim southwest to find wide canyons, overhangs and the central peak, which tops out 5ft below the surface. Parrotfish, tangs, butterflyfish and territorial damsels nibble on the abundant algae amid lush gorgonians. Cleaner gobies and wrasses set up shop atop low-profile corals. Look for stands of golden elkhorn and staghorn coral, pillar coral and lots of solitary azure vase sponges.

Northeast of the cave is a series of deeply pitted walls that are undercut as much as 30ft in places. One section boasts three tiers, each sheltering fairy basslets, grunts, squirrelfish, spotted drums, queen and French angelfish, large crabs and lobsters. You may even surprise a resting nurse shark.

35 Flanagan Reef

Dive boats anchor in Flanagan's sandy northwest cove. The main reef is on the other side of a rocky ridge south of the cove. On calm days divers swim through a narrow slot atop this ridge. Often the slot is impassable, and groups instead round the ridge.

Keep the ridge to your left as you swim west. Just around the point a narrow cut leads beneath two small arches painted in colorful sponges. Turn right into a narrow sponge-coated slot, then up and over into a fish-filled canyon at 35ft. Squirrelfish, tangs, creole wrasses and Spanish hogfish sweep the reef, while queen angelfish and fairy basslets seek the crevices.

Behind the ridge to the east is a thick field of gorgonians and sponges. Dozens of chromis, damsels, butterflyfish, hinds, scrawled filefish and other species dart amid a broad mix of corals, including star and pillar corals and golden branches of staghorn and elkhorn. Check reef nooks for porcupinefish, spotted drums, glasseye snappers and blackbar soldierfish.

Location: Flanagan Island, east of Coral Bay

Depth Range: 5-45ft+ (2-14m+)

Access: Boat

Expertise Rating: Novice

Beyond, a series of mushroom-shaped star coral mounds at 45ft shelter orange elephant ear sponges and lots of lobsters. If you have time, explore a seaward reef that slopes to about 80ft, a good place to find passing rays, turtles and pelagics.

The shallow cove is the perfect depth for a safety stop and snorkeling. Look for sand-dwelling species such as stingrays, lizardfish and goatfish, which use chopstick-like barbels to root in the sand for invertebrates. Scattered boulders are capped with gorgonians, algae and low-profile corals, which attract blue chromis, damsels and trumpetfish. Check beneath the boulders for more lobsters.

St. Croix Dive Sites

At 80 sq miles (207 sq km), St. Croix is the big sister to her northern siblings, though its population is only slightly larger than that of St. Thomas. Dotted with Danish-era plantation, sugar mill and rum factory ruins, the largely rural landscape features rolling hills as well as long stretches of grazing land for sheep, goats and native-bred Senepol cattle.

Most of the annual rain falls atop mountains to the northwest, supporting a tropical forest crisscrossed by winding roads and hiking trails. On the arid East End is Point Udall, the easternmost point in the U.S. Dominating the south side are the airport and the sprawling HOVENSA oil refinery and coker facility, one of the world's largest oil processing plants. Connected by the territory's only full-fledged highway, the main towns are Christiansted, on the north shore, and Frederiksted, on the west end.

Christiansted is the government seat and center of commerce and nightlife on the island. Overlooking the turquoise harbor is Fort Christiansvaern, its marigold walls composed of paving stones carried as ballast on Danish sailing ships. Adjacent to this national historic site is the waterfront, lined with covered pedestrian arcades that offer clothing and gift shops, several lively bars and restaurants, as well as the diving and snorkeling operators.

Lining the wharf along Christiansted Harbor, Christiansted is the center of activity on St. Croix.

North shore dive sites stretch from Buck Island to Hams Bluff, featuring lush reeftops, steep pinnacles, deep canyons and the celebrated wall, which plunges more than 2 miles (3km) into the Virgin Trough. Travel times to the sites average 10 to 45 minutes from Christiansted, while dive operators out of Salt River Marina and Cane Bay offer shorter boat rides to the more remote sites.

As Christiansted's harbor is too shallow to accommodate larger cruise ships, that honor falls to Frederiksted, on St. Croix's weather-shielded west end. This

Buck Island Reef National Monument

Five and a half miles (9km) northeast of Christiansted, Buck Island is one of the USVI's most precious natural resources. An elkhorn coral barrier reef rings two-thirds of the island. Stretching clockwise from northwest to southeast, this natural wall shelters a shallow lagoon. Though not considered a prime dive destination, these  waters offer some of the territory's most rewarding snorkeling, with healthy gorgonians, dozens of reef fish species and the occasional passing turtle or ray. The island itself is a rookery for endangered brown pelicans and a nesting site for endangered hawksbill, leatherback and green sea turtles.

Based out of Christiansted and Green Cay Marina, a half dozen park-licensed concessionaires offer half- and full-day boat trips to the island, with access for disabled visitors. The trip out takes between 40 and 90 minutes. Boats stop at West Beach, where you can swim, practice your snorkeling skills, sunbathe and picnic. Hikers may follow a winding footpath to the top of the island for views of the surrounding reef. You'll also visit the east end lagoon, where a signposted underwater trail offers snorkelers an introduction to reef ecology.

If you can't resist a peek at the reef on scuba, make arrangements through **Mile Mark Watersports**, the sole licensed dive concessionaire to the island (773-2628, www.milemarkwatersports.com). Just inside the reef to the north are two moorings set aside for scuba diving. From the lagoon, divers venture through gaps in the reef to a series of coral mounds. You'll have plenty of bottom time, as the maximum depth is only about 40ft (12m).

Concessionaires provide snorkeling gear and flotation devices, along with basic snorkeling instruction. Plan to bring a picnic lunch, your swimsuit, towel, sunglasses and waterproof sunblock. Hikers should bring shoes and bottled water. For more information call the NPS office in Christiansted (773-1460).

sleepy little outpost only fully awakens on cruise ship days, about twice a week, when shopkeepers along Strand Street open their doors and turn up the Calypso music. Cannons atop blood-red Fort Frederiksted point out at the pier and often pond-still waters beyond.

A half dozen dive operators visit the west end sites. Perhaps the most spectacular site is the pier itself, which offers fascinating night dives amid colorful and bizarre critters. To the north are the collected wrecks of Butler Bay, featuring no fewer than five ships and an underwater habitat. South of the pier is a string of healthy reefs stretching to Sandy Point National Wildlife Refuge, an important nesting ground for endangered leatherback turtles.

St. Croix Dive Sites

	Good Snorkeling	Novice	Intermediate	Advanced
36 Scotch Bank		●		
37 Long Reef		●		
38 Twin Anchors (Jason's Anchors)			●	
39 Little Cozumel			●	
40 Salt River Canyon (East & West Walls)			●	
41 Gentle Winds	●	●		
42 Rustoptwist			●	
43 Pinnacle (Jimmy's Surprise, Seamount)				●
44 Pavilions			●	
45 Cane Bay	●		●	
46 North Star	●		●	
47 Davis Bay (Carambola)	●		●	
48 Vertigo				●
49 Hams Bluff			●	
50 Butler Bay Wrecks			●	
51 Sprat Hole		●		
52 Frederiksted Pier		●		
53 King's Reach Reef & Swirling Reef of Death			●	

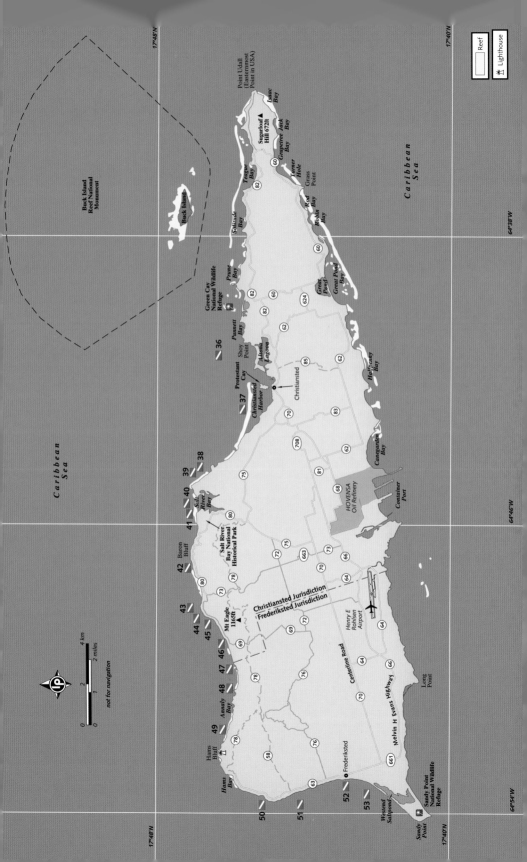

36 Scotch Bank

Stretching from the mouth of Christiansted Harbor toward Buck Island, Scotch Bank reportedly earned its name after a grounded Danish-era ship dumped its cargo of scotch while trying to float off the reef. Parched local divers insist there are still bottles to be found. Strong currents often sweep the site, dropping visibility on the reeftop. In such conditions, your boat crew may opt to drift dive the steep reef slope.

Location: NE of Christiansted Harbor

Depth Range: 30-85ft+ (9-26m+)

Access: Boat

Expertise Rating: Novice

The mooring is in 30ft of water atop the sand. Scattered coral mounds shelter hinds, lobsters, nurse sharks and large triton's trumpet mollusks, which emerge at night to feed on sea cucumbers and sea stars. Check the sand for goatfish, lizardfish and undulating sand tilefish.

Swim northwest about 100ft to reach the lip of the wall, fringed with a mix of gorgonians and rope sponges in colors ranging from green to red and purple. All the common reef species are present. Mixed chromis swirl atop colorful spheres of starlet, great star and brain corals, while filefish and trumpetfish hide amid the gorgonians.

The slope supports giant barrel and purple stovepipe sponges, as well as 5ft freestanding orange elephant ear sponges. Pretty green-tinted black corals and long strands of green and red wire corals mark the deep end of the reef, which peters out into sand at 85ft, a good turnaround point. The wall quickly plummets below 300ft, so watch your gauges and reserve plenty of air for the return to the boat.

Closer to the dock is **19th Hole**, an anchorage featuring similar depths and topography.

A graysby ducks out of the current behind an orange elephant ear sponge.

37 Long Reef

Forming a protective barrier on the north side of Christiansted Harbor, Long Reef curves west for about 3 miles. The outer reef offers several moored sites that make perfect second dives for boats returning from the north shore wall. The sites may experience strong surge, especially in winter months, which may drop visibility somewhat.

Location: North side of Christiansted Harbor

Depth Range: 15-100ft+ (5-30m+)

Access: Boat

Expertise Rating: Novice

Kaleidoscopic invertebrates draw this French angelfish to one of many swim-throughs on Long Reef.

A spur-and-groove system extends seaward and features mushroom-shaped mountainous and lobed star coral mounds, the odd staghorn, sheet and cactus corals, as well as scattered pillar and finger corals, which extend their polyps during the day to feed. Recent hurricanes have largely destroyed the once common elkhorn corals, whose battered stumps litter the shallows.

In places the star coral mounds form dramatic undercuts that shelter orange icing and elephant ear sponges, shoaling silversides, fairy basslets, grunts, angelfish, squirrelfish, snappers and lobsters. Black durgons, blue chromis, creole wrasses and blue tangs sweep the reeftops. Surprises include spotted drums, smooth trunkfish and redspotted hawkfish, which hunker down in lobed star coral mounds. Watch the blue for passing turtles, rays and large pelagics.

Closest to the harbor is **Eagle Ray**, a well-defined spur-and-groove reef that slopes from the mooring in 30ft to sandy depths below the sport-diving limit. Keep an eye out for passing eagle rays, as well as large stingrays. Rope and purple stovepipe sponges sprout from the slope, and engine parts from a small boat wreck litter a sand channel just west of the mooring.

The popular **Blue Chute** offers low-profile coral spurs and a wreck known as **Chez Barge**. From the mooring swim northeast down a wide sand chute to reach the barge. About 50ft wide and 150ft long, the upside-down barge was sunk here in the late 1970s as an artificial reef. It lies perpendicular to the slope and bottoms out in the sand at 100ft. Dive shops take groups here on fish-feeding excursions, where you

might meet Marlboro the barracuda and Earl, a rather aggressive big green moray. Marlboro often greets divers at the mooring, while Earl lives beneath the wreck and will likely come looking for you.

Named for the Water & Power authority plant visible on shore, **WAPA Garden** features mounds of undercut mountainous star corals with loosely defined channels that bottom out at 55ft.

Farthest west is **Love Shack**, or **Green Shack**, probably named for a beach shack within sight of the mooring. The site features a high-profile spur-and-groove slope that drops to a sand channel at 65ft. Seaward is another long reef that parallels the shore, followed by a mini wall.

38 Twin Anchors (Jason's Anchors)

Divers have found more than two dozen anchors along the north shore wall, lost over the centuries by visiting cargo and passenger ships. The two here are among the easiest to access. One sits in plain sight at 40ft atop the reef, while the other is deeply embedded in the wall of a nearby channel.

You'll find the first anchor less than 100ft southeast of the mooring, amid a field of fuzzy white finger corals and bright yellow cleaner wrasses. The classic iron spade hook is about 8ft long and 5ft wide, with a prominent ring that once held a heavy anchor chain. Pass it and drop down into the first sand channel. A short swim northeast is the heavily encrusted second anchor, on the left at about 55ft. Have your divemaster point it out.

Mountainous star corals dominate the spur-and-groove reef, towering above

Location: Between Long Reef & Salt River Point

Depth Range: 40-75ft (12-23m)

Access: Boat

Expertise Rating: Intermediate

deep sand valleys like a miniature Alps. After finding the anchors, meander amid the high-profile spurs, which shield you from any currents. Orange elephant ear sponges coat the undersides of many star corals, which span the channels in some spots, offering interesting swim-throughs. Check beneath them for nurse sharks, lobsters, golden crinoids, fairy basslets and wide-eyed porcupinefish.

Spend the remainder of your dive taking in the lush gorgonians and wide variety of sponges, particularly giant barrels and solitary azure vases. You'll find the usual reef species, including chromis, butterflyfish and black durgons. Watch the blue for any surprises, such as passing rays or sharks.

Once you've found the iron spade hooks, go in search of other highlights at Twin Anchors.

39 Little Cozumel

At the heart of this fun site is an east-facing box canyon about 70ft wide with a gorgonian-lined back slope and 20 to 25ft high sides. Max depth here is only 70ft on the sandy canyon floor, so this makes a perfect second dive. Exposed to offshore swells, the site is sometimes swept by strong surge and currents.

The mooring pin is at 45ft atop the canyon's south side, which drops to a mini wall that inspired the site name. It sports several species of sponges, from encrusting to black ball, azure vase, elephant ear and giant barrel. Fairy basslets skim the face both right side up and upside down.

Location: Just east of Salt River Point

Depth Range: 35-70ft (11-21m)

Access: Boat

Expertise Rating: Intermediate

The north spur is deeply undercut, its underside coated with encrusting sponges, cup corals and deepwater sea fans. Sea plumes, sheet corals, tube sponges and hydroids grow from its face, alongside an unusual sea-green octo-coral whose polyps extend to feed on plankton carried by the current. Silversides fill the undercut.

A thriving reef slope extends southeast from the canyon, featuring lots of sea rods and low-profile coral heads. Mixed chromis, bicolor damsels, cleaner wrasses and grunts stick close to the reef, while black durgons and creole wrasses rush by in a blur. Trumpetfish lurk amid the sea rods. Check reef nooks for squirrelfish, soldierfish, lobsters and eels. Look beneath larger coral mounds to find orange elephant ear sponges and pink *Stylaster* hydrocorals, whose delicate branches fan down from the undercuts.

White Horse Rock

A shallow rocky plateau just east of Salt River Canyon, White Horse is pounded by strong currents and surge that make this an advanced dive. It's only diveable on the year's few flat calm days. The site boasts one of the few stands of healthy elkhorn corals in the territory—many other stands of this top-heavy reef-building coral have fallen victim to hurricane surge. Other attractions include seahorses, sailfin blennies and such shipwreck relics as anchors, cannons and ballast. Maximum depth is about 25ft (8m).

40 Salt River Canyon (East & West Walls)

Salt River Canyon is at the mouth of a saltwater estuary, home to a mangrove lagoon and the namesake marina. On the west bank is a small beach where Spanish sailors landed during Columbus' exploration of the region in 1493. The area is protected within the Salt River Bay National Historical Park & Ecological Preserve. Diving is split between the spectacular east and west walls of the canyon, which plunge several hundred feet from shallow reeftops.

Swirling atop both walls are blue chromis, black durgons and creole wrasses. The latter boast telescoping jaws that pop from their mouths as they feed on drifting plankton. Healthy reeftop gardens shelter tangs, damsels, butterflyfish, goatfish, parrotfish, cleaner gobies and wrasses. Look amid gorgonians to spot trumpetfish, whitespotted filefish, spotted trunkfish and honeycomb cowfish, and check reef nooks for rock beauties and angelfish, fairy basslets, blackbar soldierfish, moray eels, lobsters, arrow crabs and golden

Location: Mouth of Salt River Bay

Depth Range: 30-130ft+ (9-40m+)

Access: Boat

Expertise Rating: Intermediate

crinoids. Jacks and snappers cruise the perimeter.

Moorings mark two sites on the East Wall. The inshore mooring sits atop **Russ' Rock**, an undercut mound that rises from 65ft to within 35ft of the surface. The mound is capped with sea rods and plumes, deepwater sea fans and barrel and rope sponges. Fish rush through a narrow chimney down to its base. Below the mound, reef patches sport sponges, wire corals and black corals. While the sandy slope drops well below the sport-diving limit, you'll find most life above 100ft.

From the mound a largely undercut ridge leads northwest to the point.

Search the ledges to find resting turtles. The point itself is a swirling, flashing ball of mixed reef species. Lose yourself among them as you round the corner. Divers often spot dolphins at the mouth of the canyon. They may use the estuary as a nursery for their young.

The outer mooring marks **Barracuda Bank**. Capping the wall is a sandy ridge fringed with sea rods and giant barrel sponges. Barracuda will shadow you throughout the dive. The wall slope is dotted with gorgonians and sponges, including orange elephant ear and red volcano species. Below 100ft you'll find wire corals, deepwater sea fans and black corals. Blue water surprises have included hammerhead sharks.

A quarter mile away is the West Wall, boasting the more dramatic formations. Inshore of the mooring is **Columbus' Bluff**, where millennia of limestone reef deposits have sloughed down the steep wall to form a mind-boggling maze of deep slots and towering pinnacles. Broad sheet corals are stacked along the slope amid black corals and long strands of red and lime green wire corals. Filling in the gaps are scattered coral heads and a variety of sponges, including long purple stovepipes, branching and brown tubes, ropes and giant barrels. Orange icing sponges rim several star corals.

Known by some dive crews as **Grouper Grotto**, the deeply pitted outer wall drops from 25 to 60ft, then slopes into the deep. Along the slope, mushroom-shaped coral heads form a jumble of pinnacles, canyons, overhangs and swim-throughs. The mounds are sheathed in sheet corals, deepwater sea fans, wire corals and a mix of sponges, including orange elephant ears, azure vases and purple stovepipes. Barracuda and big groupers lurk in the shadows, while ceros and rays shoot by in the blue.

Both walls feature healthy corals and sponges in a bewildering mix of shapes and colors.

U/W Photo Tips

There are several important things you can do before, during and after a dive trip to increase your enjoyment and success in underwater photography.

Before Your Trip

Take photography classes and workshops to learn the basics and hone your skills. Before purchasing an expensive system, consider renting the equipment first to try it out. If you have your own camera gear, when packing for your trip assemble the complete system at home and check that the strobes fire, the film advances and that everything works. Then disassemble it all and pack so that you don't forget any essential pieces.

If you're traveling with two camera systems, pack one complete system in its own case. That way you'll have all the needed parts if one bag doesn't arrive. If you can't carry on all your camera gear, pack the rest in a well-padded ice chest (which can also double as a rinse bucket). Remove film canisters from their boxes and pack them into a clear storage bag.

Charge all batteries the day or night before your dive. Prepare the camera beforehand and avoid rushing through the assembly. Double-check that batteries are charged, that film advances and that all controls can be read and adjusted.

Before choosing a dive operator, try and ascertain how "photo friendly" it is. Do they provide freshwater rinse buckets for camera gear on the boat? Are they happy to hand cameras down to you in the water? Can you dive alone or with other photographers? Are they flexible about working with you on your dive plan?

At the Dive Site

Bring your completely assembled cameras and ice chest/rinse bucket onto the boat. If your budget allows, bring two different cameras, each set up for a different type of photography—macro and wide angle, for example. Be sure to carry extra film and batteries onboard. If you're using a digital camera, use at least a 128MB memory card.

On the Dive

Once onboard, secure a safe spot for your camera out of the sun and away from heavy or sliding equipment. Local knowledge is vital. If the dive briefing doesn't cover the basics, ask your divemaster about unique marine subjects that may be encountered here. You should also be given a good overview of the site's general topography.

Enter the water and have your camera handed to you. Check all watertight connections before immersing the camera. Turn the camera on and check camera and strobe settings. Try to be the first one in the water.

Once on the bottom, slow down, relax and become aware of all your surroundings. Don't chase marine life, let it approach you. Search, don't swim. It's better to cover a small area thoroughly rather than a larger area quickly. Ask the divemaster to lead you to the most target-rich areas of the dive so you can maximize your shooting potential. Avoid shooting in turbid or stirred-up areas and be careful not to disturb the water near you. No picture is worth injuring yourself or marine life. Don't keep other divers waiting for you at the end of the dive.

After the Dive

Rinse or soak cameras in the rinse bucket immediately after the dive. Dry the camera and yourself well before changing film, memory cards or batteries. Be an asset, not a detriment, to the entire diving group.

— *Steve Simonsen*

41 Gentle Winds

Gentle Winds is a broad spur-and-groove reef featuring large heads of brain, mountainous and lobed star corals and big sponges. The spurs rise from the sand at 70ft and climb above 30ft well inshore. This makes a nice second dive or snorkeling site, as most features are relatively shallow and there's a lot to see.

Spaced some 15 to 30ft apart, the narrow grooves are lined with mountainous star corals. Orange icing and elephant ear sponges coat the undersides, which shelter fairy basslets, feathery golden crinoids and glasseye snappers. Check the sand for tilefish and bridled gobies.

In addition to the brain and star corals, the reeftop sports great star, finger and saucer-shaped cactus corals. You'll also find giant barrel and rope sponges. All the common reef species are present, as well as a few surprises. Rock

Location: Just west of Salt River Canyon

Depth Range: 40-70ft (12-21m)

Access: Boat

Expertise Rating: Novice

beauties purse their mouths at passing divers, while redspotted hawkfish peek from the coral mounds. Keep alert for passing turtles, rays and pelagics such as silvery African pompano.

Near the base of the mooring is a particularly large star coral mound dubbed "Gingerbread House" by local divemasters. The rare black brotula calls this mound home. Looking like a cross between a jawfish and an eel, this reclusive fish is a common sight on night dives.

42 Rustoptwist

This spur-and-groove reef lies offshore from a defunct shrimp hatchery, whose

Location: Offshore from Estate Rustoptwist

Depth Range: 30-100ft+ (9-30m+)

Access: Boat

Expertise Rating: Intermediate

intake pipes remain, snaking down the grooves into the deep. Sea rods, fans and plumes dominate the shallow reeftop, which borders a gently sloping wall anchored by mountainous star corals and big sponges. The wall descends below the sport-diving limit, but you'll find most corals and fish above 100ft.

Have your divemaster point out the seahorses.

On the reeftop, chromis, damsels and cleaner wrasses hover atop low-profile star, starlet, brain and finger corals. You may also spot smooth trunkfish and scrawled filefish. Near the mooring at 30ft is a sponge-covered rock that looks just like a seahorse—have your divemaster point it out. A short swim away you'll find the resident seahorses, which shelter within the gorgonians.

Swim north along a sand chute to the lip of the wall, patrolled by black durgons, creole wrasses, schoolmasters and yellowtail snappers. The corals here are bigger, featuring undercut mountainous star corals that span the grooves, forming delicate arches. Look beneath them to spot large porcupinefish, fairy basslets and spiny lobsters. Below 90ft the star corals give way to sheet corals, black corals, colorful wire corals and deepwater sea fans.

Sponges are also in abundance, including giant barrel, orange elephant ear, azure vase, rope, tube and purple stovepipe sponges. Lucky divers may spot passing eagle rays.

43 Pinnacle (Jimmy's Surprise, Seamount)

Your bottom time will be limited at this spectacular site, which centers on a deepwater pinnacle and adjacent undercut ledges. Perched on the lip of the north shore wall, the seamount reaches from 90 to 60ft. From its base the wall slopes to oceanic depths. Often-raging currents make this an advanced dive.

From the mooring at 55ft a ridge leads north across a field of gorgonians, sponges and low-profile corals. Looming out of the deep, the pinnacle is an impressive sight, its sides blanketed in deepwater sea fans, like a forest in winter. Bushy black corals and spindly green and red wire corals wreathe the seamount, which is capped with several very large orange elephant ear and giant barrel sponges. A ribbon of black durgons spans the water column, while cleaner wrasses spin a bright yellow ball atop the

Location: 1 mile (1.6km) NE of Cane Bay

Depth Range: 55-130ft+ (17-40m+)

Access: Boat

Expertise Rating: Advanced

Barrel sponges and deepwater sea fans sprout from the depths.

peak. Check its undercut base to find blackbar soldierfish, dozens of fairy basslets, large lobsters and resting nurse sharks. Horse-eye jacks, Nassau groupers, rock beauties and big queen and gray angels round out the field.

Just east of the pinnacle is an equally impressive series of large mounds and ledges, also deeply undercut and blanketed in deepwater sea fans. If your dive computer allows, at least check the undercuts for hiding sharks and lobsters. Monitor your depth carefully, as the formation bottoms out below the sport-diving limit and it's easy to stray too deep.

44 Pavilions

If you like to go deep but are intimidated by strong currents and sheer walls, this site is for you. Pavilions is on the eastern approach to Cane Bay, where the wall turns toward shore, affording the site some protection from ocean swells. The slope drops gently northwest, cut through by sandy paths and chutes. Below 100ft the reef dissolves into sand—make that your turnaround point.

From the mooring at 35ft make your way down one of the sand chutes, lined with mountainous and great star, starlet, pillar and brain corals. These give way to

Location: Just NE of Cane Bay

Depth Range: 35-100ft+ (11-30m+)

Access: Boat

Expertise Rating: Intermediate

sheet corals, black corals and long green and red whip corals. Sessile life is big here, featuring thick sea rods, broad sea fans, sofa-sized barrel sponges, long purple stovepipe sponges and tangled

Sponges of every description grow together in thick tangles along the reef slope.

clusters of brown tube sponges. You'll also find volcano, vase, branching tube and colorful rope sponges.

Most fish stay above 60ft, including the common chromis, tangs, damsels and wrasses. Glance overhead to spot passing black durgons, yellowtail snappers and Bermuda chub. Observant divers may find trumpetfish amid the sea fans, Caribbean spiny lobsters in deep reef crevices and spotted morays holed up in tube sponges.

45 Cane Bay

The north shore wall extends from Salt River Canyon west to Hams Bluff, but the stretch off Cane Bay beach is the best known, boasting a vertical drop, great snorkeling, thousands of fish and visibility that often exceeds 100ft. There are several ways to access the site—from the boat mooring, as a drift dive east from neighboring **Twin Palms** or from shore via Cane Bay Dive Shop.

From the boat ramp it's a hundred-yard paddle north to the swimming buoy. Thick pillars of lobed star corals rise like ancient trees from the lip of the reef. Fringed with swaying gorgonians and rope sponges, each massive coral head is a self-contained community. Mixed chromis, damsels, butterflyfish, cleaner wrasses, gobies and lots of juveniles flit atop the corals. Look beneath to find orange icing sponges, fairy basslets, squirrelfish and blackbar soldierfish.

Drop down into one of the deep sand channels that spill over the rim. You'll emerge on the sheer face and fall into the blue with outspread limbs. Watch your gauges and remember to gaze back up the wall. Lucky divers may see an eagle ray or turtle glide over the lip through long shafts of golden sunlight. The wall boasts black, wire and frilly sheet corals amid rope, tube, barrel, stovepipe and elephant ear sponges. Passing overhead are squadrons of black durgons, creole wrasses, jacks, snappers and lone barracuda.

Location: Just offshore from Cane Bay beach

Depth Range: 25-130ft+ (8-40m+)

Access: Boat or shore

Expertise Rating: Intermediate

Swim east at 80ft to find a trio of iron spade anchors inside a wide V-shaped

Anchors protrude from the wide reef buttress.

sand chute, and look for seahorses in a freestanding coral head atop the chute. Farther east are two more anchors, then only sand, with lots of garden eels and yellowhead jawfish. Spend the end of your dive off-gassing in the coral gardens or swimming back underwater toward the beach.

46 North Star

In the shadow of 1,165ft Mount Eagle, this site offers nearshore snorkeling, a small cave, a Danish-era anchor and more of the stunning north shore wall. The mooring is in 30ft on the lip of the wall, which drops almost vertically. As with many north shore sites, winter winds can make diving here difficult.

Location: .5 mile (.8km) west of Cane Bay

Depth Range: 30-130ft+ (9-40m+)

Access: Boat

Expertise Rating: Intermediate

From the field of lobed star corals beneath the mooring, swim north over the lip, passing schools of chromis, black durgons, creole wrasses and blue tangs. The anchor lies just below a small cave at 60ft. Long purple stovepipe sponges sprout from the wall above the cave, which is shared by silversides, fairy basslets and a resident green moray.

Northeast of the cave the wall is terraced with white-rimmed sheet corals and sand chutes that drop into indigo water. The gaps are filled with sea plumes, red and green wire corals and a range of sponges. Keep the wall to your right and you'll soon reach a seamount crowned in sheet and black corals. Watch your depth, as the mount peaks at 115ft and drops below the sport-diving limit. Keep an eye out for passing horse-eye jacks, cubera snappers and hawksbill turtles. The first divers down may spot blacktip reef sharks.

The reeftop sports a wider variety of corals. Just east of the mooring is a particularly large undercut star coral mound known as "The Mushroom." You'll also find lush gorgonians and lots of rope sponges. Masked gobies and myriad juvenile reef fish dart atop the coral heads, while the crevices shelter hinds, blackbar soldierfish, golden crinoids, lobsters, nurse sharks and moray eels.

47 Davis Bay (Carambola)

Divers and snorkelers access this site by boat or from shore through Anchor Dive Center's shop at Carambola Beach resort. Typical of north wall sites, Davis Bay features a spur-and-groove reef that leads to a steep drop-off. West of the mooring are sand chutes edged in brain and star corals, while to the east mountainous star corals tower dramatically over deep grooves.

Location: Offshore from Carambola Beach resort

Depth Range: 25-100ft+ (9-30m+)

Access: Boat or shore

Expertise Rating: Intermediate

From the mooring at 25ft drop into one of the sand chutes and head for the deep face, covered in sheet corals. You'll find gorgonians in the shallows and wire corals and sponges the deeper you go. Especially noticeable are orange elephant ear sponges, which grow beneath undercut star corals and in flat freestanding mounds. There's little to see but sand below 100ft.

The usual suspects dwell on the reeftop, including chromis, damsels, tangs, parrotfish, black durgons and creole wrasses. The sand channels are home to soldierfish, squirrelfish, groupers, spotted and yellow goatfish, stringy spaghetti worms, lobsters and foraging southern stingrays. Keep an eye out for passing jacks, snappers, mackerel and the odd turtle or shark.

The healthy spur-and-groove reef lies a short swim from shore at Carambola Beach resort.

48 | Vertigo

This is a site for calm days and calmer divers. Few dive boats venture this far west. Advanced divers only should make arrangements through Cane Bay Dive Shop. The anchorage overlooks the ruins of a sugar mill on the green west end slopes—a bright setting that belies the dark abyss looming below.

Location: Between Davis & Annally Bays

Depth Range: 50-130ft+ (15-40m+)

Access: Boat

Expertise Rating: Advanced

Boats hook to the reef in anywhere from 50 to 70ft of water—still considered the reeftop at this very deep site. You'll drop down into a steep, wide sand bowl that spills over the lip of the wall at 85ft. The shocker is that the wall folds back in on itself, which leaves you dangling over a hundred fathoms of inky black ocean. You'll quickly reach 130ft, the wall curling out of sight just below you, beckoning you deeper. Resist the temptation—the nearest recompression chamber is a painful plane ride away on St. Thomas.

Several wide sand chutes cut a bulging reef buttress capped by mounds of star corals and swaying gorgonians. A steel line drapes down one chute and disappears into the void. The face is coated in bushy black corals, scalloped sheet corals, red and green wire corals, bright yellow convoluted barrel sponges and tangled brown tube sponges.

Clouds of creole wrasses, black durgons and cleaner wrasses drift atop the wall, while the face shelters darting fairy basslets and blue chromis. Check the blue water for passing jacks, snappers, big pelagics and bigger sharks. You'll arrive at the surface with few adequate words to express your amazement.

Watch your gauges carefully as you slip over the edge.

49 Hams Bluff

At the foot of a rocky shoreline, this site offers lots of variety, from a gorgonian-rich slope to a maze of shallow boulders and caves. Big swells often sweep the coast, making the caves off-limits. Few operators venture here, due to the swells and proximity to shore. Make arrangements through Cane Bay Dive Shop.

Location: Just east of Hams Bluff lighthouse

Depth Range: 15-75ft (5-23m)

Access: Boat

Expertise Rating: Intermediate

From the back reef at 25ft, swim north over a short ridge, then make your way west across a hilly seascape of sand patches and coral mounds. Mountainous and great star corals rise amid sheet corals, gorgonians and a mix of sponges. Some mounds lie out from the main reef at 70ft, their sides sporting deepwater sea fans.

You'll always find chromis, damsels, tangs, parrotfish and several butterflyfish species. The mounds and ridge wall are deeply undercut, sheltering blackbar soldierfish, fairy basslets and lobsters. Surprises include green morays, as well as nurse sharks, often in the company of remoras. These torpedo-shaped fish use flat suckers on their heads to hitch rides on big fish and sometimes divers—a harmless though bizarre experience.

Return along the shallow back reef, a jumble of boulders in less than 15ft. Elkhorn corals are mounting a come-back here. You'll sway to and fro in the surge with tangs, bar jacks and big groupers. Watch for fire coral. At one point the wall dips back into twin tunnels that surface in a boulder-strewn pool. Only enter during calm conditions.

Big green moray eels meander amid the undercut mounds.

50 Butler Bay Wrecks

Butler Bay more than makes up for the dearth of diveable wrecks elsewhere off St. Croix. These waters shelter no fewer than five ships and an underwater habitat. There are two distinct sites—the two deep wrecks and the four shallow wrecks. Conditions are nearly always favorable, as the bay lies off the island's leeward west end. Check the sand for stingrays, garden eels, sand tilefish and sea cucumbers and beware encrusting fire coral, hydroids and fire worms on the wrecks' upper reaches. Several large barracuda cruise between the wrecks.

Location: 2.5 miles (4km) north of Frederiksted

Depth Range: 20-110ft (6-34m)

Access: Boat

Expertise Rating: Intermediate

The deepest wreck is the *Rosaomaira*, a 177ft Venezuelan freighter. While off-loading cinder blocks at the container port on the south side, her cargo shifted and she capsized. Still inverted, she was towed to Butler Bay and deliberately sunk in April 1986, rolling back upright as she sank. While the propeller rests in sand at 110ft, you'll spend most of your time exploring the superstructure, which tops out at 70ft. Lush growth features colorful convoluted barrel, rope and stovepipe sponges along the ship's railings, encrusting corals and sponges on the hull and black and wire corals on the deepest sections. Resident fish life includes blue chromis, blackbar soldierfish and large mutton and mahogany snappers. Check beneath the bow ramp, where big French, queen and gray angels swim amid a tangle of black corals.

Within sight of the freighter at 80ft is the latest addition to Butler Bay, the 83ft Hess Oil tug *Coakley Bay*, sunk here as an artificial reef in April 1999. While coral and sponge growth is still limited, the tug features intact windows and

The *Rosaomaira* is painted with brilliant sponges.

instruments in the wheelhouse and machinery on deck.

The shallow wrecks lie within a few hundred feet of each other in depths ranging from 45 to 85ft. Tours move counterclockwise, starting with the 123ft North Sea trawler *Suffolk Maid*. After running aground beside the Frederiksted Pier during Tropical Storm Klaus in 1984, the ship was towed here and sunk the following year. The superstructure was removed, but divers can enter the open holds for a look at the ship's machinery, ladders and other tangled wreckage. The hull is coated in cup corals and sponges, and long rope sponges sprout from the deck. Creole wrasses often sweep the ship from end to end, and a large green moray may make an appearance.

A short swim southwest is the 300ft Hess Oil barge *Virgin Islander*, sunk here as an artificial reef in March 1991. This largest of the wrecks is oddly the least interesting, as growth is limited to fire coral and tiny fans of pink *Stylaster* coral in deep recesses. Pause to look for fish and stingrays beneath the ship and glance through narrow deck slots into the sealed cavernous hold.

Continue southwest to the underwater research habitat *Aegir*, named for the Norse god of the sea. In 1970 *Aegir* housed a team of six divers for six days at a record 520ft (158m) off the coast of Hawaii. The habitat was brought to St. Croix, fell into disrepair and was sunk as an artificial reef in the late 1980s. About 30ft long and 10ft in diameter, the hourglass-shaped habitat consists of an inner sphere flanked by short tubular sections. It's an easy swim through the sections. Sponges encrust the wreck, but you'll find more life on adjacent coral mounds than in the habitat itself.

Finishing the circle due east is a 75ft oceangoing tug. The former *Witservice III*

Explore the open holds and encrusted hull of the *Suffolk Maid*, a former North Sea trawler.

was renamed *Northwind* for use as a movie prop in *Dreams of Gold: The Mel Fisher Story.* The aging vessel was sunk here following filming in 1986. You'll have plenty of time to explore, as the ship rests at 50ft and tops out at 20ft. Divers may penetrate the main hold, tour the engine room and exit up through the wheelhouse. Large sponges grow on many surfaces, including black ball, rope and purple stovepipe on the prop and forward deck and convoluted barrel on the bow. Mixed snappers, hinds and fairy basslets hide in the recesses, while chromis, sergeants, damsels and wrasses fill the water atop the wreck.

Armageddon Plain

In 1989 Hurricane Hugo pounded St. Croix, doing irreparable damage to the old Frederiksted Pier. Cherished by divers for their gorgeous coating of encrusting organisms, the battered pilings were barged a few hundred yards southwest of Butler Bay's shallow wrecks and sunk in water between 85 and 115ft deep. Local divers named the site Armageddon Plain to reflect their sense of loss. Though you'll find lots of marine life, it will take years for the pilings to return to their former glory. Boats anchor atop **Truck Lagoon**, a jumble of Hess Oil trucks sunk here in the '70s as an artificial reef.

51 Sprat Hole

This site lies just offshore from the U.S. Naval Reserve at Estate Sprat Hall. Boats moor on a bulbous orange buoy normally reserved for visiting warships. Its stout chain leads down to the sand at 35ft. West of the mooring a broad sand cul-de-sac slopes to 55ft, surrounded on

Location: Offshore from Estate Sprat Hall

Depth Range: 25-55ft (8-17m)

Access: Boat

Expertise Rating: Novice

three sides by a living city of lobed star corals in staggered depths.

Protected by its position on the lee side of the island, the site shelters particularly healthy hard corals. Amid the lobed star corals are tall mounds of great and mountainous star corals, staghorn and finger corals, spherical brain and starlet corals, and flat purplish cactus corals. Completing the scene are rope, branching tube and giant barrel sponges and swaying sea plumes.

A sandy plain skirts the craggy jumble of mixed star corals.

Darting atop the coral heads is the usual mix of chromis, cleaner wrasses, damsels and tiny masked gobies, as well as passing parrotfish and creole wrasses. Peer beneath the corals to find orange elephant ear sponges, jewel-like fairy basslets, blackbar soldierfish, hinds, squirrelfish and glasseye snappers, as well as banded coral shrimp and Pederson cleaner shrimp. Look for long white strands of what looks like angel hair pasta. They belong to aptly named spaghetti worms, which withdraw into the reef if disturbed.

Lucky divers may see spotted scorpionfish, smooth trunkfish and pairs of whitespotted filefish. Don't overlook the sand flats, which are home to goatfish, stingrays and a large colony of garden eels. Rosy razorfish perch on the sand, darting beneath it in a flash if approached too closely.

52 Frederiksted Pier

Despite the loss of the old pier, this remains a magical site, especially at night. Opened in 1994, the new concrete and steel pier extends 1,526ft into calm Frederiksted Bay. The favorite entry point is a short hop off the dinghy dock, followed by a leisurely surface swim out to the end of the pier. Steer clear of locals' fishing lines as you paddle out. Bright dock lights make navigation easy.

On your way out, stop for a peek at the old pier's dolphins—stacked concrete pilings used as mooring fenders. One look at the incredible sponge growth and you'll appreciate local divers' sense of loss. Don't linger long, though, as the new pier offers plenty to see.

As you thread through the pantheon of pilings, take care to avoid the dozens of fire worms. Piles of scattered debris shelter octopuses and goldentail moray eels, while lobsters form conga lines, latching together for safety as they cross the sand. Look closer to spot such gems as highhats, frilly fileclams and grape-sized juvenile smooth trunkfish. The eagle eyes among you will find seahorses, spotted scorpionfish

Location: Frederiksted Harbor

Depth Range: 15-50ft+ (5-15m+)

Access: Shore

Expertise Rating: Novice

and even the rare roughback batfish, with its garish red lipstick smear of a mouth. Huge tarpon prowl the well-lit perimeter.

A safety stop is unnecessary, as the seafloor gradually rises toward shore. As

A rare find, roughback batfish live beneath the pier.

you reach the shallows, shine your dive light amid the boulders to spot golden-eyed shrimp and resting parrotfish, which snooze in self-made mucus sleeping bags. Watch your footing as you exit over slick concrete slabs.

53 King's Reach Reef & Swirling Reef of Death

The seascape between Frederiksted and Sandy Point drops in terraces to oceanic depths. King's Reach Reef takes in the first terrace, starting at a sandy anchorage in 45ft of water and sloping west to a sandy plateau at 100ft. Vast colonies of garden eels bookend the slope. These snakelike eels hover vertically out of their burrows, feeding on current-borne plankton. As you approach, they'll retreat beneath the sand in unison.

Location: .5 mile (.8km) SW of Frederiksted

Depth Range: 45-100ft (14-30m)

Access: Boat

Expertise Rating: Intermediate

Covering the slope are stovepipe, rope and tube sponges, 5ft orange elephant ears, bright yellow branching tubes and hot tub–sized barrel sponges. Corals include lobed, mountainous and great star, brain, starlet and cactus atop the reef, with sheet and wire corals in deeper water. Farther south you'll find larger lobed and mountainous star coral mounds. Blackbar soldierfish school openly in daylight here, alongside chromis, butterflyfish, angelfish, gobies and wrasses.

Back on the reeftop, scattered coral patches alternate with wide sand flats. Spaghetti worms extend threadlike white tentacles from beneath the corals. Look carefully to find spotted drums and rock hinds, and check the sand for peacock flounders, goatfish and nearly transparent bridled gobies.

Farther inshore is the Swirling Reef of Death (formerly **Dan's Reef**). Renamed by an overimaginative young diver, this healthy patch reef lies in less than 40ft of water. You can perch in one spot for the entire dive, watching dozens of adult and juvenile reef fish atop mounds of corals and sponges. Look closer to spot goldentail and chain morays. Patient divers can pause for a manicure from Pederson cleaner shrimp. Tigertail sea cucumbers reach from beneath the reef, looking like an elephant's trunk in search of a peanut.

Nocturnal blackbar soldierfish emerge in daylight along the slope.

Marine Life

The Virgins' warm, tropical waters are home to more than 500 species of fish, 40 types of coral and hundreds of invertebrates. Juvenile reef fish start life amid seagrass beds and the sprawling roots of nearshore mangroves. They move out to reefs capped with corals, sponges and swaying gorgonians. Brittle stars and arrow crabs shelter within the sponges, while deeper recesses shelter lobsters, moray eels and large nurse sharks. Watch the blue water to spot passing jacks, turtles and lone pelagics.

Following is a photo gallery of common vertebrates and invertebrates you'll likely see. The next section describes potentially hazardous species you may encounter.

Keep in mind that common names are used freely by most divers and are often inconsistent. The two-part scientific name is more precise. This system is known as binomial nomenclature—the method of using two words (shown in italics) to identify an organism. The first italic word is the genus, into which members of similar species are grouped. The second word, the species, refers to a recognizable group within a genus whose members are capable of interbreeding.

Common Vertebrates

sand diver
Synodus intermedius

longspine squirrelfish
Holocentrus rufus

blackbar soldierfish
Myripristis jacobus

Nassau grouper
Ephinephelus striatus

fairy basslet
Gramma loreto

redspotted hawkfish
Amblycirrhitus pinos

109

horse-eye jack
Caranx latus

yellowtail snapper
Ocyurus chrysurus

porkfish
Anisotremus virginicus

bluestriped grunt
Haemulon sciurus

French grunt
Haemulon flavolineatum

spotted drum
Equetus punctatus

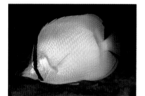

spotfin butterflyfish
Chaetodon ocellatus

rock beauty
Holacanthus tricolor

queen angelfish
Holacanthus ciliaris

blue chromis
Chromis cyanea

yellowtail damselfish
Microspathodon chrysurus

sergeant major
Abudefduf saxatilis

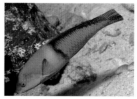

creole wrasse
Clepticus parrae

yellowhead wrasse
Halichoeres garnoti

princess parrotfish
Scarus taeniopterus

yellowhead jawfish
Opistognathus aurifrons

sharknose goby
Gobiosoma evelynae

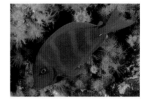

blue tang
Acanthurus coeruleus

queen triggerfish
Balistes vetula

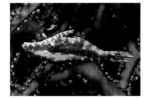

slender filefish
Monacanthus tuckeri

porcupinefish
Diodon hystrix

Common Invertebrates

deepwater sea fan
Iciligorgia schrammi

pillar coral
Dendrogyra cylindrus

Christmas tree worm
Spirobranchus giganteus

flamingo tongue
Cyphoma gibbosum

common octopus
Octopus vulgaris

Caribbean reef squid
Sepioteuthis sepioidea

yellowline arrow crab
Stenorhynchus seticornis

Pederson cleaner shrimp
Periclimenes pedersoni

spiny brittle star
Ophiocoma paucigranulata

Hazardous Marine Life

Marine animals almost never attack divers, but many have defensive and offensive weaponry that can be triggered if they feel threatened or annoyed. The ability to recognize hazardous creatures is a valuable asset in avoiding injury. The following are some of the potentially hazardous creatures most commonly found in the Virgin Islands.

Shark

Sharks come in many shapes and sizes. They are most recognizable by their triangular dorsal fin. Though many species are shy, there are occasional attacks. According to the International Shark Attack File, in the past century there have been only four recorded shark attacks in VI waters. About 25 species worldwide are considered dangerous to humans. Sharks will generally not attack unless provoked, so don't taunt, tease or feed them. Avoid spearfishing, carrying fish bait or splashing excessively, and your likelihood of being attacked will greatly diminish. Face and quietly watch any shark that is acting aggressively and be prepared to push it away with a camera, knife or tank. If a fellow diver is bitten by a shark, stop the bleeding, reassure the patient, treat for shock and seek immediate medical aid.

Barracuda

Barracuda are identifiable by their long, silver, cylindrical bodies and razorlike teeth protruding from an underslung jaw. They swim alone or in small groups, continually opening and closing their mouths, an action that looks daunting but actually assists their respiration. Though barracuda will hover near divers to observe, they are really somewhat shy, though they may be attracted by shiny objects that resemble fishing lures. Irrigate a barracuda bite with freshwater, and treat with antiseptics, anti-tetanus and antibiotics.

Moray Eel

Distinguished by their long, thick, snakelike bodies and tapered heads, moray eels come in a variety of colors and patterns. Don't feed them or put your hand in a dark

hole—eels have the unfortunate combination of sharp teeth and poor eyesight, and will bite if they feel threatened. If you are bitten, don't try to pull your hand away suddenly—the teeth slant backward and are extraordinarily sharp. Let the eel release it and then surface slowly. Treat with antiseptics, anti-tetanus and antibiotics.

Stingray

Identified by its diamond-shaped body and wide "wings," the stingray has one or

two venomous spines at the base of its tail. Stingrays like shallow waters and tend to rest on silty or sandy bottoms, often burying themselves in the sand. Often only the eyes, gill slits and tail are visible. These creatures are harmless unless you sit or step on them. Though injuries are uncommon, wounds are always extremely painful, and often deep and infective. Immerse wound in nonscalding hot water and seek medical aid.

Jellyfish

Jellyfish sting by releasing the stinging cells contained in their trailing tentacles. As

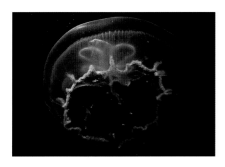

a rule, the longer the tentacles, the more painful the sting. Stings are often irritating and not painful, but should be treated immediately with a decontaminant such as vinegar, rubbing alcohol, baking soda, papain, or dilute household ammonia. Be aware that some people may have a stronger reaction than others, in which case you should prepare to resuscitate and seek medical aid.

Fire Coral

Although often mistaken for stony coral, fire coral is a hydroid colony that secretes a hard, calcareous skeleton. Fire coral grows in many different shapes, often encrusting or taking the form of a variety of reef structures. It is usually identifiable by its tan, mustard or brown color and fingerlike columns with whitish tips. The entire colony is covered by tiny pores and fine, hairlike projections nearly invisible to the unaided eye. Fire coral "stings" by discharging small, specialized cells called nematocysts. Contact causes a burning sensation that lasts for several minutes and may produce red welts on the skin. Do not rub the area, as you will only spread the stinging particles. Cortisone cream can reduce the inflammation, and antihistamine cream is good for killing the pain. A doctor should treat serious stings.

Bristle Worm

Also called fire worms, bristle worms can be found on most reefs. They have segmented bodies covered with either tufts or bundles of sensory hairs that extend in tiny, sharp, detachable bristles. If you touch one, the tiny stinging bristles lodge in your skin and cause a burning sensation that may be followed by a red spot or welt. Remove embedded bristles with adhesive tape, rubber cement or a commercial facial peel. Apply a decontaminant such as vinegar, rubbing alcohol or dilute ammonia.

Sea Urchin

Sea urchins tend to live in shallow areas near shore and come out of their shelters at night. They vary in coloration and size, with spines ranging from short and blunt to long and needle-sharp. The spines are the urchin's most dangerous weapon, easily able to penetrate neoprene wetsuits, booties and

gloves. Treat minor punctures by extracting the spines and immersing the area in nonscalding hot water. More serious injuries require medical attention.

Scorpionfish

Scorpionfish are well-camouflaged creatures that have poisonous spines along their dorsal fins. They are often difficult to spot since they typically rest quietly on the bottom or on coral, looking more like rocks. Practice good buoyancy control, and watch where you put your hands. Scorpionfish wounds can be excruciating. To treat a puncture, wash the wound and immerse it in nonscalding hot water for 30 to 90 minutes.

Diving Conservation & Awareness

Reefs in the USVI have suffered considerable damage in the past quarter century. Natural causes have had the greatest impact, notably coral diseases and damage from repeated hurricanes and tropical storms. White band disease and storm damage alone have reduced elkhorn coral coverage at Buck Island Reef National Monument from 85% to less than 5%.

Human activity also plays a role. According to the Global Coral Reef Monitoring Network, about one-fifth of reef loss in the Caribbean is due to anchor damage, boat groundings, sewage bypass and runoff from shoreline development. Overfishing also remains one of the primary threats to marine life. Researchers have noted a link between overfishing of herbivorous species and a boost in algal growth on the reef, which in turn smothers corals.

Marine biologists have attempted to transplant live corals to stimulate development and speed recovery, but the damaged reefs are slow to regenerate. Also at risk are mangroves and seagrass beds, which provide shelter and food to a number of marine species.

Much valuable research has come out of the UNESCO-MAB Biosphere Reserve Center's Caribbean Field Station in Virgin Islands National Park on

Sahara Dust

Hurricanes aren't the only atmospheric phenomenon that links the Caribbean with North Africa. The same strong easterly trade winds that spawn cyclonic storms off the coast of Africa also pick up sand particles from the Sahara Desert and carry them across the Atlantic to the Caribbean. So-called "Sahara dust" is visible in the air as haze. While the haze makes for spectacular sunsets, researchers have suggested a link between certain coral diseases and fungal spores borne aloft in the dust. The dust may also play a role in the frequency and intensity of hurricanes in the region.

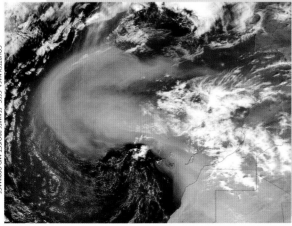

COURTESY NASA, GSFC, SEAWIFS PROJECT AND ORBIMAGE

St. John, established to study conservation techniques. For the past decade U.S. Geological Survey biologists from the field station have been using photography, digital video and satellite imagery to monitor the health of reefs and fish life in park waters around St. John and Buck Island off St. Croix. Further research will be used to develop marine conservation strategies worldwide.

Marine Reserves & Regulations

Local and federal agencies have established a vast network of parks, monuments, wildlife refuges and marine reserves to protect more than 50,000 acres (20,000 hectares) of land and waters in the USVI. Three parks form the core of that protection. Encompassing some three-fifths of St. John, Virgin Islands National Park was created in 1956 and expanded to include 5,650 acres (2285 hectares) in surrounding waters. First protected in 1948, Buck Island off St. Croix was proclaimed a national monument in 1961. An executive order in 2001 expanded the monument to include an additional 18,000 acres (7,285 hectares) of submerged land. The legislation also set aside the new 12,708-acre (5,145-hectare) Virgin Islands Coral Reef National Monument off St. John.

Not everyone is thrilled with the protected areas, however, notably those in the commercial fishing industry, who are barred from large no-take fishing zones throughout the territory. And on St. John there is continued pressure to develop private land and reopen roads within Virgin Islands National Park. Such development could increase runoff and further damage nearshore reefs. The opposing groups must achieve a sustainable balance between commercial needs and ecological pressures.

To meet demand from increased boat traffic, dive operators and the NPS have installed more than 300 moorings in USVI waters over the past decade. Patrolling in a fleet of Boston Whalers, NPS rangers enforce regulations and maintain more than 200 moorings in VINP waters and another dozen moorings off Buck Island. Since 1995 the Reef Ecology Foundation has installed some 75 moorings in non-park waters around St. Thomas and St. John. St. Croix dive operators started Project Anchors Away in 1989, installing 22 moorings along the island's north shore. The group was recently awarded a grant to install another 50 moorings. These programs rely on private donations and government grants, not to mention the efforts of dive operators and park rangers to maintain the moorings.

Responsible Diving

Dive sites are often along reefs and walls covered in beautiful corals and sponges. It only takes a moment—an inadvertently placed hand or knee, or a careless brush or kick with a fin—to destroy this fragile, living part of our delicate ecosystem. By following certain basic guidelines while diving, you can help preserve the ecology and beauty of the reefs.

1. Never drop boat anchors onto a coral reef, and take care not to ground boats on coral. Encourage dive operators and regulatory bodies in their efforts to establish permanent moorings at appropriate dive sites.

2. Practice and maintain proper buoyancy control and avoid overweighting. Be aware that buoyancy can change over the period of an extended trip. Initially you may breathe harder and need more weighting; a few days later you may breathe more easily and need less weight. Tip: Use your weight belt and tank position to maintain a horizontal position—raise them to elevate your feet, lower them to elevate your upper body. Also be careful about buoyancy loss: As you go deeper, your wetsuit compresses, as does the air in your BC.

3. Avoid touching living marine organisms with your body and equipment. Polyps can be damaged by even the gentlest contact. Never stand on or touch living coral. The use of gloves is not recommended: Gloves make it too easy to hold on to the reef, damaging the coral. The abrasion caused by gloves may be even more damaging to the reef than your hands. Steady yourself in the sand, or if you must hold on to the reef, use only your fingertips on exposed rock or dead coral.

4. Take great care in underwater caves. Spend as little time within them as possible, as your air bubbles can damage fragile organisms. Divers should take turns inspecting the interiors of small caves or under ledges to lessen the chances of damaging contact.

5. Be conscious of your fins. Even without contact, the surge from heavy fin strokes near the reef can do damage. Avoid full-leg kicks when diving close to the bottom and when leaving a photo scene. When you inadvertently kick something, stop kicking! It seems obvious, but some divers either panic or are totally oblivious when they bump something. When treading water in shallow

National Park Regulations

Following is a list of NPS regulations governing all park waters and land. For more information visit or call the park visitor centers in Cruz Bay on St. John (776-6201) or Christiansted on St. Croix (773-1460).

- It is illegal to remove coral, sea fans or shells from park waters
- Do not touch, break or stand on coral
- It is illegal to dump litter in park waters or on land
- Do not disturb or remove natural or historical features
- It is illegal to disturb turtle-nesting sites
- Do not feed or approach wild donkeys
- Do not touch or taste unfamiliar plants
- Water skis, boogie boards and JetSkis are prohibited
- Spearguns are prohibited
- Beach fires are prohibited

reef areas, take care not to kick up clouds of sand. Settling sand can smother the delicate reef organisms.

6. Secure gauges, computer consoles and the octopus regulator so they're not dangling—they are like miniature wrecking balls to a reef.

7. When swimming in strong currents, be extra careful about leg kicks and handholds.

8. Photographers should take extra precautions, as cameras and equipment affect buoyancy. Changing f-stops, framing a subject and maintaining position for a photo often conspire to thwart the ideal "no-touch" approach on a reef. When you must use holdfasts, choose them intelligently (i.e., use one finger only for leverage off an area of dead coral).

9. Resist the temptation to collect or buy coral or shells. Aside from the ecological damage, collection of marine souvenirs depletes the beauty of a site and spoils other divers' enjoyment.

10. Ensure that you take home all your trash and any litter you may find as well. Plastics in particular pose a serious threat to marine life.

11. Resist the temptation to feed fish. You may disturb their normal eating habits, encourage aggressive behavior or feed them food that is detrimental to their health.

12. Minimize your disturbance of marine animals. Don't ride on the backs of turtles or rays, as this can cause them great anxiety.

Marine Conservation Organizations

Coral reefs and oceans face unprecedented environmental pressures. The following groups are actively involved in promoting responsible diving practices, publicizing environmental marine threats and lobbying for better policies:

CORAL: The Coral Reef Alliance
☎ 510-848-0110
www.coral.org

Coral Forest
☎ 415-788-REEF
www.blacktop.com/coralforest

**Environmental Association of
St. Thomas–St. John (EAST)**
☎ 776-1976
www.usvi.net/east

Friends of Virgin Islands National Park
☎ 779-4940
www.friendsvinp.org

Project Anchors Away
toll-free ☎ 800-235-9047
or 800-532-3483
(Michelle Pugh or Laurie Dunton)

Project AWARE Foundation
☎ 714-540-0251
www.projectaware.org

Ocean Futures
☎ 805-899-8899
www.oceanfutures.com

Reef Ecology Foundation
www.reefecologyfoundation.org
info@reefecologyfoundation.org

**Reef Environmental Education
Foundation (REEF)**
☎ 305-451-0312
www.reef.org

ReefKeeper International
☎ 305-358-4600
www.reefkeeper.org

Listings

Telephone Calls

To call someone in the Virgin Islands, dial the international access code of the country you are dialing from (not necessary from the U.S. or Canada) + 340 (the territory's area code) + the local 7-digit number. Toll-free 800, 866, 877 and 888 numbers are accessible from the U.S. and, usually, Canada.

Diving Services

Dive centers in the USVI are typically well run and offer an array of services. All provide a full range of rental scuba gear, including masks, fins, snorkels, wetsuits, weight belts, BCs, regulators and tanks. Many also sell complete lines of scuba equipment and accessories. Several rent underwater cameras, and a few offer nitrox to properly certified divers.

All centers offer dive training and certification, including resort courses for the uninitiated. Some have been trained by the Handicapped Scuba Association (HSA) to provide courses and tours to the disabled. A few offer DPV (diver propulsion vehicle, or underwater scooter) tours of the reefs, allowing you to cover much more ground on your dive.

Following is a list of reputable dive centers on all three islands.

St. Thomas

Admiralty Dive Center
Holiday Inn Windward Passage
P.O. Box 307065
Charlotte Amalie
St. Thomas, VI 00803
☎/fax: 777-9802
toll-free ☎ 888-900-3483
www.admiraltydive.com
admiralty@viaccess.net
Dive boats: *M2R Duck* (30ft monohull), *CM Duck* (25ft monohull), *MR Duck* (23ft monohull)
Passenger capacity: 12, 6 and 6, respectively
Courses: (NAUI, PADI) Open Water through Divemaster; specialties
Other: Cater to small groups by expertise level; Spanish-speaking; handicapped training and dives; DPV tours

Aqua Action Dive Center
Secret Harbour Beach Resort
6501 Red Hook Plaza, #2
St. Thomas, VI 00802
☎ 775-6285 fax: 775-1501
toll-free ☎ 888-775-6285
www.aadivers.com
aquaaction@islands.vi
Dive boat: *Nina* (27ft monohull)
Passenger capacity: Licensed for 16, limited to 10
Courses: (PADI) Open Water through Divemaster; specialties
Other: Offer handicapped training and dives; kayak rentals

St. Thomas (continued)

Barefoot Adventures
Best Western Carib Beach Resort and
Best Western Emerald Beach Resort
P.O. Box 9438
St. Thomas, VI 00801
☎/fax: 776-3140 or ☎ 775-2040, ext. 5020
toll-free ☎ 866-362-2220 or
800-233-4936, ext. 5800
www.barefootoutfitters.com
barefootoutfitters@hotmail.com
Dive boat: *Barefoot Diver* (30ft monohull),
Jaws (44ft monohull)
Passenger capacity: 15 and 6, respectively
Courses: (PADI) Open Water through
Divemaster; specialties
Other: Specialize in West End and North Side
sites; equipment storage and cleaning for
resort guests; kayak and trimaran rentals

Blue Island Divers
Suite 505, Crown Bay Marina, Sub Base
St. Thomas, VI 00802
☎ 774-2001 fax: 777-9600
www.blueislanddivers.com
diveusvi@islands.vi
Dive boat: *Island Diver* (28ft monohull)
Passenger capacity: Licensed for 17,
limited to 8
Courses: (PADI) Open Water through
Divemaster; (BSAC) Ocean Diver through
Advanced Instructor; specialties and skill
development courses
Other: Cater to small groups; nitrox avail-
able; access remote reefs and wrecks

Chris Sawyer Diving Center
American Yacht Harbor Complex (Red
Hook), Renaissance Grand Beach Resort,
Wyndham Sugar Bay Resort and Compass
Point Marina
6300 Estate Frydenhoj
Suite 29
St. Thomas, VI 00802
☎ 777-7804, 775-7320 fax: 775-9495
toll-free ☎ 877-929-3483
www.sawyerdive.vi
sawyerdive@islands.vi
Dive boats: 45ft monohull and *Fool's Gold*
(42ft monohull)
Passenger capacity: 18 and 12, respectively
Courses: (NAUI, PADI) Open Water through
Divemaster; specialties
Other: In business since 1982; cater to small
groups; weekly trips to RMS *Rhone* in BVIs

Coki Beach Dive Club
Coki Beach
P.O. Box 502096
St. Thomas, VI 00805
☎/fax 775-4220
toll-free ☎ 800-474-2654
www.cokidive.com
pete@cokidive.com
Courses: (PADI) Open Water through
Divemaster; specialties
Other: Steps from the beach and nearshore
reef; personalized attention; adjacent to
Coral World marine park

Dive In
Sapphire Beach Resort & Marina
P.O. Box 503180
St. Thomas, VI 00805
☎ 777-5255 fax: 777-9029
toll-free ☎ 866-434-8346
www.diveinusvi.com
divein@attglobal.net
Dive boat: *Challenge* (32ft monohull)
Passenger capacity: Licensed for 16,
limited to 10
Courses: (PADI) Open Water through
Divemaster; specialties
Other: Offer dedicated snorkeling excur-
sions; daytrips to BVI; extensive watersports
rentals

Hi-Tec Watersports
East Gregerie Channel
P.O. Box 2180
Sub Base
St. Thomas, VI 00803
☎ 774-5650
Other: Professional testing and repair;
equipment for rent/sale; airfill station

St. Thomas Diving Club
Bolongo Bay Beach Club & Villas
7147 Bolongo Bay
St. Thomas, VI 00802
☎ 776-2381 fax: 777-3232
toll-free ☎ 877-538-8734
www.st-thomasdivingclub.com
bill2381@viaccess.net
Dive boats: *Elysian Lady* (48ft catamaran),
Letts Dive (30ft monohull), *La Bateau* (27ft
monohull)
Passenger capacity: 20, 10 and 6, respectively
Courses: (PADI, NAUI, SSI) Open Water
through Instructor
Other: PADI 5-Star IDC; nitrox available;
weekly trips to RMS *Rhone* in BVIs

St. Thomas (continued)

Underwater Safaris
Yacht Haven Marina
5300 Long Bay Road
St. Thomas, VI 00802
☎ 774-1350 fax: 777-8733
www.diveusvi.com
uws@islands.vi
Dive boats: *Tropic Diver* (45ft catamaran),
Reef Safari (45ft catamaran)
Passenger capacity: 49 on each
Courses: (PADI) Open Water through
Instructor; specialties
Other: PADI 5-Star IDC; books tours,
parasailing, sailing, etc.

WaterWorld Outfitters
Havensight Mall and Marriott Frenchman's
Reef Beach Resort
Building 7C
Havensight Mall
St. Thomas, VI 00802
☎ 774-3737 fax: 774-3738
www.diveusvi.com
wwo@islands.vi
Dive boat: *Eagle Ray* (45ft catamaran)
Passenger capacity: 49
Courses: (PADI) Open Water through
Assistant Instructor; specialties
Other: Books tours, parasailing, sailing, etc.

St. John

Cruz Bay Watersports
Cruz Bay and Westin Resort
P.O. Box 252
St. John, VI 00831
☎ 776-6234 and 693-8000 (ext. 1833/4)
fax: 693-8720
www.divestjohn.com
info@divestjohn.com
Dive boats: *Island Time* (59ft monohull),
Blast (40ft monohull), *Sea Quest* (38ft
monohull), *Splash* (25ft monohull)
Passenger capacity: 60, 18, 14 and 6,
respectively
Courses: (PADI, NAUI) Open Water through
Assistant Instructor
Other: Offer dedicated snorkeling trips and
demos; daytrips to BVIs; watersports rentals;
free snorkeling map at both locations

Low Key Watersports
Wharfside Village, Cruz Bay
P.O. Box 716
St. John, VI 00831
☎ 693-8999 fax: 693-8987
toll-free ☎ 800-835-7718
www.divelowkey.com
lowkey@viaccess.net
Dive boats: *Hey Now* (36ft monohull),
Low Key (36ft monohull)
Passenger capacity: 26 and 22, respectively
Courses: (PADI, NAUI, SSI) Open Water
through Instructor; specialties
Other: PADI 5-Star IDC; offer private instruc-
tion and charters; weekly trips to RMS
Rhone in BVIs; kayak and dinghy rentals

Maho Bay Watersports
Maho Bay
P.O 1152
St. John, VI 00831
☎ 776-6226, ext. 239
toll-free ☎ 800-392-9004, ext. 239
www.maho.org/diving.html
mbws@viaccess.net
Dive boat: *Ocean Quest* (32ft monohull)
Passenger capacity: Licensed for 14,
limited to 10
Courses: (PADI) Open Water through
Divemaster; specialties
Other: Only operator within Virgin Islands
National Park; relaxed diving schedule;
dedicated snorkeling excursions; extensive
watersports rentals

Paradise Watersports
Caneel Bay
P.O. Box 1554
St. John, VI 00831
☎/fax: 779-4999 or 774-5295
www.paradisevi.com
paradiseh2o@attglobal.net
Dive boats: *Big Dog* (38ft monohull),
Bad Dog (34ft monohull)
Passenger capacity: Big Dog (licensed for 26,
limited to 10), Bad Dog (licensed for 14,
limited to 8)
Courses: (PADI, NAUI) Open Water through
Divemaster; specialties
Other: Cater to small groups; specialize in
private charters; nitrox available

St. John (continued)

St. John Dive Adventures
Coral Bay
P.O. Box 9901
St. John, VI 00830
☎ 714-7273
toll-free ☎ 866-771-3483
www.stjohndiveadventures.com

info@stjohndiveadventures.com
Dive boat: *Laura Leigh* (32ft monohull)
Passenger capacity: 6
Courses: (PADI) Open Water referrals
Other: Specialize in East End sites; cater to small groups; dedicated snorkeling excursions; daytrips to BVIs

St. Croix

Adventures over the Edge
Frederiksted Hotel
442 Strand St.
Frederiksted
St. Croix, VI 00840
☎/fax: 772-0505 fax: 772-0500
www.frederikstedhotel.com/diveshop.htm
aote@viaccess.net
Dive boat: *Dive World* (21ft monohull)
Passenger capacity: 6
Courses: (PADI) Open Water through Instructor; specialties
Other: PADI 5-Star IDC; specialize in West End sites; offer dedicated snorkeling tours; Spanish-speaking

Anchor Dive Center
Salt River Marina, Carambola Beach
P.O. Box 5588
Sunny Isle
St. Croix, VI 00823
☎/fax: 778-1522
toll-free ☎ 800-532-3483
www.anchordivestcroix.com
info@anchordivestcroix.com
Dive boats: *Splash* (33ft monohull), *Queen B* (26ft monohull), *Buoyancy* (20ft monohull)
Passenger capacity: Splash (licensed for 17, limited to 10); Buoyancy, Queen B (6)
Courses: (PADI) Open Water through Divemaster; specialties
Other: Sole operator licensed to dive Buck Island; DPV tours; kayak rentals

Cane Bay Dive Shop
Cane Bay Beach, Frederiksted and Christiansted
P.O. Box 4510
Kingshill
St. Croix, VI 00851

☎ 773-9913 fax: 778-5442
toll-free ☎ 800-338-3843
www.canebayscuba.com
canebayscuba@viaccess.net
Dive boats: *Seawasp I* (20ft catamaran), *Seawasp II* (20ft catamaran)
Passenger capacity: 6 per boat
Courses: (PADI) Open Water through Divemaster; specialties
Other: Specialize in private diving and snorkeling charters; unlimited shore diving packages; nitrox available; rebreather training and rentals; kayak rentals

Dive Experience
Comanche Building
40 Strand St.
P.O. Box 4254
Christiansted
St. Croix, VI 00822
☎ 773-3307 fax: 773-7030
toll-free ☎ 800-235-9047
www.diveexp.com
divexp@viaccess.net
Dive boat: *Dive Experience II* (28ft monohull)
Passenger capacity: 15
Courses: (PADI, NAUI, SSI) Open Water through IDC; specialties
Other: PADI 5-Star IDC; in business since 1983; offer fish-feeding trips

Mile Mark Watersports
59 King's Wharf
P.O. Box 3045
Christiansted
St. Croix, VI 00822
☎ 773-2628 fax: 773-9411
dive-stcroix@worldnet.att.net
Other: Snorkeling excursions to Buck Island

St. Croix (continued)

Scuba Shack
72-B La Grande
P.O. Box 3221
Frederiksted
St. Croix, VI 00841
☎/fax: 772-3483
www.stcroixscubashack.com
dave@stcroixscubashack.com
Dive boat: *Gizmo* (20ft monohull)
Passenger capacity: 6
Courses: (PADI, NAUI) Open Water through
Divemaster; specialties
Other: Specialize in West End sites; cater to
small groups; short boat trips; night dives at
Frederiksted Pier

Scubawest
330 Strand St.
Frederiksted
St. Croix, VI 00840
☎ 772-3701 fax: 713-1459
toll-free ☎ 800-352-0107
www.divescubawest.com
adventure@divescubawest.com
Courses: (PADI) Open Water through
Divemaster; specialties
Dive boats: *Up and Under* (30ft monohull),
Afternoon Delight (40ft monohull), *Narcosis*
(20ft monohull)
Passenger capacity: *Up and Under*
(licensed for 20, limited to 13); *Narcosis*,
Afternoon Delight (6)
Other: Specialize in West End sites; cater to
small groups; short boat trips; night dives at
Frederiksted Pier

**St. Croix Ocean Recreational
Experiences/V.I. Divers**
2 Concordia
P.O. Box 6116
Kingshill
St. Croix, VI 00850

☎ 773-6045 fax: 778-4338
toll-free ☎ 877-773-6045
www.scorevi.com
score@viaccess.net
Courses: (PADI, SDI/TDI) Open through
Divemaster; specialties
Dive boats: *Tarpon Shark* (29ft monohull),
Tarpon Shark II (36ft monohull)
Passenger capacity: 6 per boat
Other: Cater to small groups; in business
since 1971; Spanish-speaking; nitrox available

St. Croix Ultimate Bluewater Adventures
Christiansted and Rainbow Beach Club
14 Caravelle Arcade
Christiansted
St. Croix, VI 00820
☎ 773-5994 fax: 773-5910
toll-free ☎ 877-567-1367
www.stcroixscuba.com
stcroixscuba@att.net
Dive boats: *Reliance* (38ft monohull), *Scuba
Deux* (17ft rigid inflatable)
Passenger capacity: 14 and 6, respectively
Courses: (PADI) Open Water through
Divemaster; specialties
Other: Personalized service; offer South
Shore excursions

The Waves at Cane Bay
P.O. Box 1749
Kingshill
St. Croix, VI 00851
☎ 778-1805 fax: 778-4945
toll-free ☎ 800-545-0603
www.canebaystcroix.com
ry1805@viaccess.net
Courses: (PADI) Open Water through
Assistant Instructor; specialties
Other: Diving services for hotel guests only;
unlimited shore diving packages;
personalized service

Cruise Lines

The majority of visitors to the USVI arrive via cruise ship. Vessels range from elegant four-masted sailing ships to multistory floating hotel-casinos that accommodate several thousand passengers. Web-based services include online booking, passenger bulletin boards, itineraries, weather reports, maps and information on meal plans, spa treatments and excursion planning.

Many cruise lines hire their own diving instructors and offer a range of confined-water certification and specialty classes in the ship's pool, with scheduled open-water dives at the island destinations. Divers can take advantage of preplanned diving excursions or phone ahead to reserve space on a local dive boat. The following are cruise lines whose ships visit the territory:

Carnival Cruise Lines
toll-free ☎ 888-227-6482
www.carnival.com

Celebrity Cruises
toll-free ☎ 800-437-3111
www.celebritycruises.com

Clipper Cruise Line
toll-free ☎ 800-325-0010
www.clippercruise.com

Costa Cruise Lines
toll-free ☎ 800-462-6782
www.costacruises.com

Crystal Cruises
toll-free ☎ 800-446-6620
www.crystalcruises.com

Cunard Line
toll-free ☎ 800-728-6273
www.cunard.com

Disney Cruise Line
toll-free ☎ 800-511-1333
www.disneycruise.com

Holland America Line
toll-free ☎ 800-426-0327
www.hollandamericaline.com

Norwegian Cruise Line
toll-free ☎ 800-327-7030
www.ncl.com

Princess Cruises
toll-free ☎ 800-774-6237
www.princess.com

Radisson Seven Seas Cruises
toll-free ☎ 800-285-1835
www.rssc.com

Royal Caribbean Cruise Line
toll-free ☎ 800-327-6700
www.royalcaribbean.com

Seabourn Cruise Line
toll-free ☎ 800-929-9391
www.seabourn.com

Silversea Cruises
toll-free ☎ 800-722-9955
www.silversea.com

Windjammer Barefoot Cruises
toll-free ☎ 800-327-2601
www.windjammer.com

Windstar Cruises
toll-free ☎ 800-258-7245
www.windstarcruises.com

Tourist Offices

The USVI Department of Tourism operates visitor centers on the three major islands, which offer tips on accommodations, restaurants, shopping, etc., with plenty of free brochures, including popular cartoony maps and weekly guides to each island. If you plan on renting a car, stop by to pick up a copy of the *Official Virgin Islands Road Map*, a detailed folding road atlas to the territory.

On St. Thomas there are visitor centers at the airport arrivals terminal, the West Indian Co. cruise ship dock and 1 Tolbod Gade, across from Vendors' Plaza/Emancipation Garden in Charlotte Amalie (774-8784). The St. John visitor center (776-6450) is in a small building beside the post office, across the street from the passenger ferry terminal. St. Croix's visitor centers are at the airport arrivals terminal, 53A Company St. in Christiansted (773-0495) and 1 Strand St. in Frederiksted (772-0357).

U.S. Virgin Islands Department of Tourism
www.usvitourism.vi
toll-free ☎ 800-372-8784

Index

dive sites covered in this book appear in **bold** type

Lonely Planet Pisces Books

The **Diving & Snorkeling** guides cover top destinations worldwide. Beautifully illustrated with full-color photos throughout, the series explores the best diving and snorkeling areas and prepares divers for what to expect when they get there. Each site is described in detail, with information on suggested ability levels, depth, visibility and, of course, marine life. There's basic topside information as well for each destination.

Also check out dive guides to:

Australia's
Great Barrier Reef

Bali & Lombok

Baja California

Bermuda

Bonaire

Chuuk Lagoon,
Pohnpei & Kosrae

Cocos Island

Curaçao

Fiji

Guam & Yap

Honduras' Bay Islands

Jamaica

Maldives

Monterey Peninsula &
Northern California

New Zealand

Pacific Northwest

Palau

Papua New Guinea

Philippines

Red Sea

Scotland

Seychelles

Southern California
& the Channel Islands

Tahiti
& French Polynesia

Texas

Thailand

Vanuatu